Start and Run a Profitable Home-Based Business

Edna Sheedy

Self-Counsel Press
(a division of)
International Self-Counsel Press Ltd.
USA Canada

Printed in Canada.

First edition: April 1990
Reprinted: June 1990; October 1990; September 1991; September 1992; July 1993
Second edition: March 1994
Reprinted: September 1994; June 1995; May 1996
Third edition: July 1997; April 1999

Canadian Cataloguing in Publication Data

Sheedy, Edna, 1939 –
  Start and run a profitable home-based business

    (Self-counsel business series)
  ISBN 1-55180-148-5

  1. Home-based businesses. I. Title. II. Series.
HD2333.S53 1997   658'.041   C97-0910313-4

Self-Counsel Press
(a division of)
International Self-Counsel Press Ltd.

1704 N. State Street	1481 Charlotte Road
Bellingham, WA 98225	North Vancouver, BC V7J 1H1
USA	Canada

To Tim, who says, "you can,"
and Patsy, who says, "you will."

Contents

Worksheets

Samples

Introduction

We work not only to produce but to give value to time.

Eugène Delacroix

The growth in home-based business in recent years has been staggering, and it shows no sign of stopping. Estimates suggest that by the year 2000, nearly 40% of the North American work force will operate from their homes. Some of this home-based work force will consist of telecommuters, corporate employees linked to their offices by home computers. Others will be experienced business people who have quit the office towers and opted instead for the less stressful surroundings that the home environment, at its best, can provide. But a large part of this work force will be new entrepreneurs — people who have decided to take a chance on themselves and their capabilities. Leaving behind the regimen of nine to five, they will blend dreams and ambitions to create vital, new home-based businesses.

Both economics and technology are contributing to this change in our economy. The economic advantages of running a business from home cannot be disputed. It *is* more cost effective. Technology has played its part by making it not only easier but increasingly more efficient to work at home.

But it is not technology or economics that created this work-at-home phenomenon. It is the result of a growing need for independence and a desire to control, as best we can, that master of us all — time. The phrase "quality time" was born in the late seventies. Such time was conserved for children, family, friends, and leisure pursuits; it was distinct from working time. Quality time was elusive, often lost completely in busy, high-pressured lives. We talked of "making time," "finding time," "getting time," and, by doing so, became acutely aware of how ineffective such efforts were. Time, we discovered, is not an expandable commodity, and we realized how little of it we had.

Quality is no longer enough; we want quantity as well. The business person has decided to reclaim this time, not purely for economic reasons but also because of a freshly discovered sense of the value of time. Now, with the tools in place, people are staying home to work in increasing numbers. They are finding new and creative routes to homemade profits. The entrepreneur has become the "homepreneur."

Every day, new businesses start in the home, and many of them are successful beyond the dreams of their founders. Sadly, many are not. The reality is that merely saving on the rent is not enough. Running your business from home requires the same drive and skills demanded of any business person. It may require even more.

Many people find working at home lonely. They miss the camaraderie of coworkers, the *esprit de corps* inherent in teamwork and shared goals. They often have difficulty managing their work day, allowing themselves to be easily distracted from the tasks at hand. The reclaimed hours are wasted, vanishing before their eyes, and they are left with a nagging sense of guilt. The homepreneur may set the clock, but the clock does its own ticking.

Working at home requires perseverance, self-motivation, and a talent for time management. Most of us do our best work under pressure, and the added responsibility of creating that pressure for ourselves can be difficult. This is particularly true in the early stages, that first year when it is necessary to plan and organize for your business's future. It can be all too easy to procrastinate and lose the critical sense of urgency required to get the business on stream and productive.

If you are planning to start a business at home, you want it to be a winner, and you want the satisfaction that comes with owning a well-run, profitable enterprise. To achieve your goal, think deeply and plan carefully. The principles of running a successful business are the same at home as they are downtown or in a factory in an industrial park. It doesn't take magic to operate a business, it takes craft — and the craft can be learned.

The raw material for business success is good judgment and common sense. By using both, you will become an informed and skillful homepreneur. The reward for your effort will be more than profits, it will be a glowing sense of accomplishment from a job well done.

This book is meant to be your ally and sidekick as you meet the challenge of your first year in business. I hope it helps.

1

On being a homepreneur

First ponder, then dare.

Helmuth von Moltke

There has never been a better time for starting a home-based business. Books, pamphlets, seminars, and television shows all tell you that you can do it. There is no shortage of technology either: answering machines, computers, cellular phones, home copiers, and facsimile processing equipment. It is all "user-friendly" and all designed to help you work where you want, when you want.

The magazine articles make it seem easy. Filled with glossy photos of people who have "made it," they urge you on. You can do it, they say — and tell 1,001 success stories to prove it. It seems everything is in place for you to jump right in, if jumping in is what you want to do.

Wait.

Is it really *that* simple? Just read a few books, hook up a fax machine, and get on with it?

Not quite.

There are things to learn along the path to business success, and aspiring homepreneurs instinctively know this. From the beginning, their minds are filled with questions. Is running a business right for them? Will it work in their home? What does a business need to reach its potential? What skills are necessary to make it profitable? What lies behind the gloss? Good questions all.

By looking past the veneer of business success, you begin to see its underpinnings, understand how it is built, and judge the strength of its pillars. You can then decide if a home-based business is for you.

Starting a business *is* easy. Making and keeping it successful are the tricky parts. It doesn't matter if your business is in the basement or a downtown high rise; failure will still be an unhappy and stressful experience. Running your business from home can minimize your financial loss, but it won't save you from depression should it flounder.

Success in business requires basic know-how. That expertise, the knowledge and skills to meet challenges and problems and overcome them, is available to everyone planning a business venture.

The first step is to think — think deeply — about yourself, your family, your home, and your ambitions. Should you decide that homepreneurship is right for you, the next step is to take action to ensure that ambition becomes reality.

A clear understanding of the risks and rewards of running your own show is a good place to start your thinking process.

a. Pros and cons

Let's take a look at the advantages and disadvantages of running a home-based business.

1. Advantages

(a) *You are the boss.* This is probably the most seductive reason of all for starting your own business. All others pale by comparison. It affords a sense of freedom and independence that no job, however rewarding, can match.

(b) *You will have a high degree of control.* This reason often appeals to the independent, creative person who is constrained by old-fashioned management and antiquated business methods.

(c) *You can benefit from tax advantages.* Purely monetary, but why give the tax department any more than you have to? The ability to deduct part of your home expense is a genuine bonus.

(d) *You have the potential for higher earnings.* In theory, as a business owner, there is no limit on what you can earn. If your business is successful, you simply give yourself a raise.

(e) *You enjoy self-fulfillment.* The personal rewards of seeing your ideas, your plans, and your work produce measurable results goes a long way to making homepreneurship worthwhile.

Business is a good game — lots of competition and a minimum of rules. You keep score with money.

Nolan Bushnell

(f) *You can create your own work environment.* This is a special benefit of working at home. If you want purple wallpaper and polka dot carpets, there is nothing to stop you (except perhaps good taste!).

(g) *You have less stress.* I prefer to say less *distress*. If you have a bad day, you're free to take a walk, stare at the wall, or simply "close your business" for an hour or so. There is nothing and no one to stop you.

(h) *You can save money.* There are no exorbitant rents to pay, no high gasoline bills, less wear and tear on the car, and, depending on the job, perhaps less wardrobe expense.

(i) *You have more time with your family.* No need for you to miss your child's first step, a parent/teacher meeting, or that "truly important" high school baseball game at 3:30 p.m. How about a stolen hour or two with your spouse? You can set your own priorities and act accordingly.

(j) *You can have flexible working hours.* Not all of us are programmed to work nine to five. In your own business at home, you choose the hours you work. If your most energetic time is between 5 p.m. and midnight, you are free to make this your working schedule. This appeals strongly to women with small children because it allows them to work while the children are at school or daycare.

2. *Disadvantages*

(a) *There will be monetary risk.* You will, like any business person, have to risk capital. If you think a business, any business, can run on air, you are mistaken. Sooner or later, cash has to go on the line. It may be only a few hundred dollars, but it can be a strain for those who are not used to it.

(b) *There will be pressure to perform.* You're on your own. This is the flip side of being your own boss. The business depends on you and you alone. This responsibility can

"ACME INC. HOW CAN I HELP YOU?"

weigh heavy if you routinely depend on others to help you out.

(c) *You will need to be an expert in a variety of tasks.* There are many tasks to accomplish in a home-based business: sales, record keeping, inventory, finance, and management to name a few. To be successful, you should develop competence in each of them. Running a successful business is a continuous learning experience.

(d) *It may be difficult to leave work behind.* Many people who work at home find it impossible to turn off the lights on their business. The time they gain from not commuting to work can be easily forfeited by staying too long at their desks.

(e) *There is the possibility of irregular income.* Business has its ups and downs. Unfortunately, your income can follow the same pattern. If you have always had a fixed income, company benefits, and paid holidays, you should expect to make sacrifices, particularly in the early stages.

(f) *You will face loneliness and isolation.* The most difficult part of running a business from your home is feeling cut off. This can be a real stumbling block if you don't take steps to handle it. If you plan an active network of business associates, such feelings can be beaten. Most homepreneurs do have to take action to overcome the sense of isolation.

(g) *You might have motivation difficulties.* It can be too easy to linger over morning coffee, putter in the garden, or go to the driving range. Lack of motivation can starve the fledgling enterprise. Motivation is an inner resource that relies on strong desire to meet your goals. It is not easily *manufactured.*

The purpose of business activity is to realize profits.

(h) *Business may stay with you after hours.* Some home-business people are burdened by customers 24 hours a day. Many customers believe that if you are working at home, you are available around the clock. They think nothing of calling well into the evening. This problem can be handled, but it will take some discipline and planning on your part.

b. *Does the shoe fit?*

An important word in the phrase "home-based business," and one that many would-be homepreneurs ignore, is "business." My old Webster's lists "purposeful activity" as an archaic definition of the word. It may be archaic, but I can't think of any better way to say it.

The purpose of business activity is to realize profits. You may not be aiming for a million-dollar bottom line, but you do want to make enough for the venture to be worthwhile. If you don't, you will soon lose interest — not to mention cash.

The profits should compare favorably to the effort expended to achieve them. Many people rush into business without giving this enough thought. When the day comes that they do, they realize they are working 15 hours a day to make $1.50 an hour. The effort expended far outweighs the cash reward. This ice-water awakening is harsh and unsettling, but it can be avoided with thought and planning.

Of course, profit takes many forms. Money is one of them. But intangibles such as enjoyment and self-fulfillment are equally important to the long-term success of your business. If you can't enjoy what you do — if your business doesn't contribute to your growth as a human being — your cash profits will be cold comfort. It is doubtful that you will enjoy being in business for yourself unless the activity fits your personality.

c. *Characteristics required for success*

What is it that makes one person succeed while another fails? Endless studies have attempted to find the answer to that question, yet it remains elusive.

While there is no stereotype of successful business people, certain characteristics are common to them. For example, they are invariably hardworking, persevering, and resourceful, and they are capable of honest self-appraisal when it is called for.

Starting with the truth about what you are good at and what you aren't gives you the chance to overcome weaknesses that may keep you from the success you seek. If you never manage your time well, procrastinate endlessly, and have real difficulty working alone, a home-based business may not be for you unless you make a serious

Almost every man wastes part of his life in attempts to display qualities which he does not possess.

Samuel Johnson

effort to overcome such tendencies. You don't have to be perfect — no one is — but it is essential that you recognize your strengths and weaknesses before you take a false step.

So, before you begin, do some self-analysis.

The following quiz (see Worksheet #1) is based on what are generally considered to be the characteristics required for success. Answer the questions to determine how many success characteristics you have. Be honest with yourself and remember, no one person has them all — all of the time. You can answer yes if that's the way you are *most* of the time.

No quiz, test, or questionnaire can definitively dictate to you what you should or should not do. Its value lies in helping you think by engaging you in honest appraisal. You are capable of capitalizing on your strengths and compensating for your weaknesses as long as you know what they are and if your passion to succeed is powerful enough.

As a homepreneur, you are often required to develop and hone skills that don't come easily, such as marketing and selling your product or service, record keeping, and time management. If you start your business with a partner, you can share these responsibilities; if not, all the responsibility rides on you. If you accept that, are secure in your self-knowledge, and eager to learn, what problems you have will be easily overcome.

Part of that self-knowledge must be a complete understanding of your reasons for wanting to be a business person in the first place. *Why do you want to start a business?*

d. Your starting point

Accurate figures on the number of home-based businesses are difficult to come by, but in Canada estimates are that close to two million people now work either full time or part time from home. In the United States, recent surveys tell us that almost 25 million people are now running some kind of business in their homes. According to *Home Business News*, a publication of the American Home Business Association, 8,000 people start a home business every day — one every 11 seconds. Many of these businesses will be wonderfully successful, fulfilling the expectations of their owners and contributing to the quality of their lives.

But some will fail.

Reasons for failure in business are many. Experts cite shortage of capital, poor business skills, and lack of sales ability as prime causes. There is another — starting a business for the wrong reasons. If your motivation arises from cloudy thinking about a glorious future where you will be rolling in money, you may be setting yourself up for disappointment.

No one likes to think about failure. It is a nasty word for a nasty circumstance, and one that we all wish vehemently to avoid. You might be asking, "Why talk about it now? I did well on the quiz, and, besides, I haven't even started my business yet." The reason is that it is a mistake to hide failure behind the door. If you want to avoid failure, it's a good idea to recognize it early in your business cycle.

You are motivated to start a business venture. Take a moment to think about why. The why of what you're doing is just as important as the how. If you are motivated to be an homepreneur by mile-high expectations, by greed, or because it looks like an easy road, chances are you won't make it, and you'll disrupt your life and household as well.

Do Worksheet #2 to help you determine your real motivation for starting your own home-based business.

Worksheet #1
Characteristics of success

Check the appropriate column for each of the following statements.
(N = never; M = most of the time; A = Always)

		N	M	A
1.	I am a self-starter.			
2.	I am normally positive and optimistic.			
3.	I easily accept personal responsibility.			
4.	I have no problem working alone.			
5.	I am competitive.			
6.	I commit strongly.			
7.	I am flexible.			
8.	I am self-confident.			
9.	I relate well to other people.			
10.	I am a goal setter.			
11.	I am a creative problem solver.			
12.	I like to plan.			
13.	I am a decision maker.			
14.	I enjoy working hard.			
15.	I can tolerate risk.			
16.	I seldom procrastinate.			
17.	I am innovative.			
18.	I handle stress well.			
19.	I am independent by nature.			
20.	I am a logical thinker.			
21.	I am persistent.			
22.	I communicate well with others.			
23.	I manage my time well.			
24.	I have a high degree of common sense.			
25.	I have the ability to think objectively.			
26.	I am in good health.			
27.	I like to learn new things.			
28.	I am realistic.			
29.	I can take criticism.			
30.	I am ambitious.			

Now determine your score. Should you start your own business at home? Count your **Always** and **Most of the time** answers as a positive. If you scored —

30 out of 30	You should be running General Motors.
26 - 29	You've got what it takes.
21 - 25	You'll do just fine.
16 - 20	Be sure you answered yes to number 14 and 27.
15	Questionable.
Under 15	Unlikely, but nothing is impossible.

Worksheet #2
Why do you want to start a business?

Circle the answers that apply to you.

I want to start a business because:

1. I just want to make money.
2. I just want more time off.
3. I need more personal achievement.
4. I hate my boss.
5. I just think it would be fun.
6. I just got fired.
7. I need a more fulfilling lifestyle.
8. I need a challenge.
9. I believe I can make a better widget.
10. I just want to work alone.
11. I need to control as much of my life as possible.
12. I believe I can better use my skills on my own.

There's no score this time, but if you picked the reasons that started with "I just," you need a new compass; your sense of direction is all wrong. On the other hand, if you were attracted to the reasons that started with "I need" and "I believe," you are on the right track. Starting your home business should be built on the strong motivation that the words *need* and *belief* imply.

Start a business to make a better widget, to challenge yourself, to enhance your lifestyle, or to control your working life. If your starting point is negative, don't. You must be motivated by strong desire, and that desire should be positive and realistic. Misguided dreams will not sustain you.

2

Choosing your business

The shoe that fits one person pinches another;
there is no recipe for living that fits all cases.

Carl Gustav Jung

If you're lucky, the business you'll be operating has chosen you. By that I mean your experience, skills, and ambition have combined to show a clear path for you to follow. You know what you want to do. You know that the business you are interested in will function within the home, and you are just now embarking on the process of learning how to do it to ensure success.

For some, the way is not so easy.

a. Some businesses to run from home

If you have only a hazy idea of the business you wish to start, you have a lot of work to do. While you have many options open to you, finding a business with strong, personal appeal that will benefit from your experience may take some thought.

Many businesses are successfully operated from the home. Here are a few examples:

- Furniture repair
- Small appliance repair
- Home renovations
- Interior design
- House painting

- Automobile repair
- Woodworking
- Daycare
- Pet care
- Catering
- Furniture manufacturing
- Consulting (e.g., business, computer)
- Training (e.g., software programs, cooking)
- Tutoring
- Book editing
- Newsletter publishing
- Desktop publishing
- Printing
- Word processing
- Distribution
- Real estate sales
- Personal services
- Accounting services
- Sewing and alterations
- Fashion design
- Clothing manufacturing

As you can see, there is no shortage of ideas for businesses that can be adapted for the home, but the best idea will ultimately be your own. Try to think of a business that not only has a good potential for profit but also holds a strong attraction for you. Think about what you really want to do. Chosen well, your business should provide financial and personal reward.

There is a saying that the way to success in business is to find a need and fill it. True, but keep in mind that our society consumes not only what it *needs* but also what it *desires*. Wants and desires are not always rational or justified. For example, I don't *need* a toaster cover that looks like a duck, but I bought one. Why? Because I *wanted* it.

There is a big difference between the words need and want, but both present opportunities for the homepreneur. The similarity is that both motivations drive the consumer to buy, whether the purchase

They say you can't do it, but sometimes it doesn't always work.

Casey Stengel

11

is rational or, like my toaster cover, not so rational. As you consider your future business, try to keep your potential customers in mind and consider how and why your product or service will appeal to them.

If the choice of your home business is not clear, take the following steps:

(a) Open your eyes — wide. Look around, observe, try to spot a service or product that is right for you and your home. Train yourself to ask whether the things you buy and use represent opportunities.

(b) Read everything you can find about small businesses, not just those currently run from the home, but others you see that could be brought to the home.

(c) List ideas that come to you. Jot them down and examine them carefully. If an idea is good, it begins to take on a life of its own. Often what starts out muddy or indistinct, given time and research, gels into a solid concept for a business.

(d) Consider your hobbies and interests. Is one of them the basis for a business? Examine your work experience. If you are currently employed, take a look at what your company buys. Business services are often initiated by people who see something their company needs and is prepared to pay for. What about your hobbies? Business publications are filled with stories of successful home businesses that started out as hobbies.

(e) Think about your present job. Is all or part of it *transportable?* Many of today's more progressive employers are open to the idea of employees working from home on a contract basis. This particularly applies to office services. What you do now might be the basis for your home-based service. Would there be other customers for your skills?

(f) Attend trade shows in your area. Tour the booths, talk to the people there, and listen. Trade shows are a direct source if you are looking for products to market. They are also a good place to find ideas if you are not sure about the direction you want to take.

(g) Subscribe to business magazines and trade journals. Pay particular attention to those targeted to small business. Often these magazines run special editions devoted to home-based business. They keep you up on current trends and may provide the spark of inspiration you're looking for.

(h) Appraise your own skills. Do you have a special skill that you could teach to others? Are you an expert in something that would allow you to work as a consultant? Services are the fastest growing segment of home-based business and, if you are talented enough, the easiest to start. Information and training is always in demand.

(i) Check the business section of your local newspaper. Write for information. Respond to franchise advertisements that target home enterprise. If you are considering franchising as an option, be sure to research what you are buying very, very carefully. Many franchisors deliver what they promise, but many do not. Before you put money on the table, check it out painstakingly.

There are many excellent reference books on franchising, so do your homework. Beware of "get rich quick" ads that promise you can make $20,000 a week, no effort required. Look out! Buy a lottery ticket instead. The odds for success are probably about the same.

Don't forget to check your local library for ideas. You'll find many books with all sorts of helpful suggestions to offer. (See Appendix 2 for a list of helpful books.)

The Internet abounds with information on home-based opportunities. If you are a user, do some surfing with research in mind. The hits, while they may not be opportunities in themselves, will stir your creative juices. But be cautious: there are a lot of questionable *offers* directed to the naive and gullible via news groups and Web sites. If you consider responding to any of them, put the brain on full alert. Unfortunately, the Net as a tool is as accessible to the shyster promoter as it is to the honest business person.

b. You, your home, and your family

The home-based business is a unique blend of family, skills, and lifestyle. To make the blend rich and prosperous, each must be considered independently. For the moment, let's concentrate on you.

1. The business and you

Business success is determined by the skill and experience of its operator. Fortunately, there are very few of us that have reached adulthood without acquiring some expertise along the way. The trick

THERE ARE FEW SMALL BUSINESSES THAT HAVEN'T GOT A STORY TO TELL ABOUT MIXING BUSINESS AND FAMILY.

Try hard to find a business that has strong personal appeal and that compliments your existing abilities.

is to categorize your abilities and put them to good use as a business person.

Before making an investment in any business, it is a good idea to identify the skills you feel most confident about and start from there. It would be foolish indeed to start a bookkeeping business if you have never kept a set of books in your life. That may seem obvious, but would-be entrepreneurs make such decisions every day.

On the other hand, no rule says you can't start a business in which you have neither past experience nor skills. It is a challenge, but it can be done. We all have an enormous capacity to learn and change. If this is the direction you plan to take, determine now to set about acquiring the skills you need before you risk time or cash on the venture. Investigate local colleges and training institutes, work in the business for someone else, subscribe to the appropriate trade magazines, and, where possible, talk to people in similar businesses. If you are determined to set a new career course, chart it with care.

Most people go with what they've got. A super salesperson can readily turn those selling skills into a home business by finding a line of products in his or her field and becoming an independent distributor. A computer expert can set up as a consultant or contract programmer. To be successful, they still have to learn and develop good business practices, but the enterprise they start is based on proven experience and recognizable skills. It's the best possible starting point. The task would be much more complicated if the computer programmer wanted to be a distributor or the salesperson wanted to teach programming.

Take the time to assess your talents and abilities. In Worksheet #3, make a list of your skills, both working and non-working, hobbies, special interests, etc. This is your chance to blow your own horn. You'll be the only one to hear it, so don't hold back. List everything. Think about what your friends or business associates say about you. Do they say how well-organized you are? That you have a talent for sales? Write it down. Outside opinion has value and can help guide

Worksheet #3
Inventory of personal skills and interests

1. My skills are:

_____

_____

_____

_____

_____

_____

2. Special interests:

_____

_____

_____

_____

_____

_____

3. What other people say I'm good at:

_____

_____

_____

_____

_____

_____

you. This is your business's first inventory of assets and perhaps its most important. As you search out and define your business opportunity, keep this list of skills and interests in mind. Try hard to find a business that has strong personal appeal and that compliments your existing abilities.

2. *The business and your home*

Is the business you've chosen suitable for your home environment? Is there sufficient space available for you to conduct your business undisturbed?

The environment you work in is important, and you need to think carefully about it. Ideally, you should run your business from a separate room where, when the work day is over, you can shut the door (and lock it if there are young, inquisitive children around the house). It can be a little-used den, a spare bedroom, the basement, or even the garage, as long as there is ample space for supplies, inventory, and record keeping. It surprises most homepreneurs how quickly the space they set aside fills to the brim with paper alone.

In the early stages of planning to run a business from home, it is worthwhile to review the physical environment that will house the new enterprise. Most residential floor plans make no allowance for running a business. It can seem a bit like trying to make a square peg fit into a round hole. Often some real innovative thinking is required to create space that will allow you to work productively and give you the privacy you need. Although organizing the home office is covered in some detail in chapter 8, now would be a good time to walk around your home and make the effort to look at it with a new pair of eyes — those of a professional business person. Think about the following:

(a) Privacy

Is there space, or can you make space, where you can work undisturbed? If the nature of your endeavor requires that it be childproof, either for the safety of the children or the protection of your business, can it be done?

Having a private work area that allows you to separate yourself both physically and visually from household responsibilities will contribute greatly to your success as a homepreneur.

When you think about privacy, think about where your business telephone will be. *The ability to have uninterrupted telephone conversations is essential to your business.* It's unlikely that you will want your three-year-old picking up that long-distance call or having a lively but unintelligible conversation with an important client.

16

Having a private work area with that all-important door between you and the rest of the household has other benefits, too. For the home business person to stay motivated, he or she must be able to separate business work time from house work time. It's difficult to concentrate on getting that report out or packaging and billing that last order if, directly in your line of vision, there is a hamper of unwashed laundry or several hundred dust bunnies crying for immediate attention. Having a private work area that allows you to separate yourself both physically and visually from household responsibilities will contribute greatly to your success as a home-preneur.

(b) Noise

Everyone has a different reaction to noise. Indeed, each person defines what he or she considers to be noise according to that reaction. Teenagers don't call the latest music played at full volume noise, but chances are their parents will — and certainly your customers will! Your computer's printer clanking away at midnight might be music to your ears, but pure torture to a tired spouse.

When it comes to the home business, there are two types of noise to think about: the noise you hear and the noise you create as you run your business. Both must be tolerable if the merging of home and business is not to cause friction. If you must work in absolute quiet, or your enterprise creates noise bothersome to the family, you might want to consider soundproofing your work area. You might also check the door that will separate business from family. Most inside doors have a hollow core that easily allows sound to pass through. Replacing such a door with a solid core door will decrease noise passing between the two areas. Often such a replacement completely solves the noise problem.

One last word about noise. From your point of view, you might think that you require absolute silence in order to work when, in fact, the opposite is true. Many people, particularly those accustomed to working in a busy office environment, actually miss the din of the office they were so anxious to leave. At least one new home business person I heard of made a tape of such office sounds. He puts it on every morning to, as he says, "just get me going." The message is that for some people, too much silence acts as a demotivator.

(c) Area

The business should also be compatible with the area you live in and cause no disruption or annoyance to your neighbors. If your business creates noise, undue traffic, or, heaven forbid, noxious fumes, your neighbors' tolerance will be tested in the extreme, and a disgruntled neighbor can be bad for business. There have been instances where area residents have been successful in closing down a home-based business that they see as having a high nuisance value.

3. *The business and your family*

(a) Child care considerations

Most often the spouse who chooses to work at home is the one with primary responsibility for child care. Blending the two tasks is no easy matter, particularly with very young children. The needs of the children and the demands of the business are often at odds with each other. Doing some advance thinking and preparing for it will help you to deal with the conflict. Understand from the beginning that simply working at home may not completely eliminate child care concerns — although at first, when the demands of the business are small and you can easily adjust your schedule to conform to that of the children, it may seem so. This could change rapidly. It is best to think about how you will handle child care well in advance of starting your business. If your children are very young, here are some options:

(a) *Working around your children's schedules:* This is probably the toughest route to take when starting a home-based business, and it is almost impossible to sustain. With no specified working time and even less planning time, chances are you will feel pressure beyond your ability to cope. By trying to operate a demanding business with no control over your own time, you can expect to eventually become bone-weary and probably bad-tempered. The business will suffer and so will your family.

Still, it must be said that some homepreneurs do operate their businesses in just this manner. They minimize the stress involved by having realistic expectations. They are successful when their financial goals are moderate and the business is not customer intensive. Often they are contract people who perform highly specialized work for select, and very understanding, clients. But if your aim is to expand your business, this option is probably not for you.

(b) *Working while children are in school:* Many home businesses are run during school hours. Five or six uninterrupted hours can be enough to operate a successful home enterprise. While this might not eliminate the need for child care during school holidays or summer vacation, it can be a valid choice for parents who want their children to hear a welcoming hello when they come home from school. This schedule can work for both service and home manufacturing businesses. Many homepreneurs manufacture only during school hours and manage to build sufficient inventory to satisfy their financial goals.

(c) *In-home care:* Many home business people have found this to be the most satisfactory method of child care, particularly if their children are still very young and their financial plan for the business is ambitious. This method of child care allows the spouse working at home to remain close to the children while still having the blocks of uninterrupted time necessary to operate the business. Having someone come to the home on a regular basis to provide consistent, reliable child care makes a very real contribution to the business and the home-preneur's peace of mind. The disadvantage of in-home child care is cost, but if your financial resources are up to it, it is the best choice.

(d) *Out-of-home care:* If you are working at home to be near your children, this means of child care may not make any sense to you. You probably didn't decide to work at home so you could send your children elsewhere. Still, many home workers do choose this method of child care — some for five days a week, some for one or two, depending on their need for quiet and the demands of their business. If you must have some uninterrupted time, and your budget is tight, this might be your only alternative.

(b) Communicating with the older child

Your need for child care while running your home business will depend on several factors, notably your financial objectives, the time required to meet those objectives, and the ages of your children. The children, regardless of age, will be affected by your decision to start and run a home-based business, so communicate as openly with them as you can. Telling older children about your plans, answering their questions, and discussing mutual concerns will help make them team players in the enterprise.

From 12 and up, children benefit greatly from frank discussion about the new business. They need to know the importance of your undertaking and what part, if any, they will play in it. There's nothing wrong with laying out a few clearly defined rules covering things such as interruptions (when and what for) and telephone etiquette. If your teenager will be answering your business phone, take some time to instruct him or her on what to say, how to say it, and how to properly record messages. Most important, older children should understand what effect your working at home will have on the family and what changes can be expected.

If you don't speak clearly about your objectives in starting the business, you may create a situation in which your children resent the new enterprise and the time you devote to it. Consciously or unconsciously, they may even act as saboteurs by making excessive demands and indulging in difficult behavior just when you need their cooperation most.

(c) Leave time for your family

For a business to merge successfully with the family, you must be able to leave it behind. Some new homepreneurs become almost obsessed with their operation and find it impossible to stop thinking or talking about it. Many find themselves going back to work after dinner, late at night, or on weekends. *For your sake and that of your family, don't turn yourself into a home workaholic.* This is another reason for that separate, self-contained work space. Closing that door at the end of your working day gives you a clear dividing line between work and family needs.

(d) Working with your spouse

If you work alongside your spouse in the business, you will need to add yet another layer of understanding to your relationship. Marriage can create stress; so can business. Put them together, and it can be too much for either partner to bear. The truth is, living and working with a spouse can be either an idyll or a nightmare. It depends on the couple and their capacity for understanding and honest dialogue. The need for communication cannot be overstressed, and neither can the need for occasional privacy for whichever spouse requires it. Many couples who work together plan and schedule at least one day a week away from each other.

Working and living together requires self-discipline. Leaving family tensions at home and business disagreements at the office is a challenge when they are under the same roof. Couples who work together successfully learn how to deal with contentious issues quickly and openly. They do not allow minor irritations to fester. Some couples find it easier to defuse potential disputes because they are in business together. Oddly enough, disagreements are often settled more readily when it can be done "for the good of the business."

Couples who do work together and are successful in forging a strong, productive relationship have the bonus of enjoying the success of the business together. For some, this reward far outweighs whatever difficulties they meet along the way.

3

Defining your goals

Hope is a good breakfast but it is a bad supper.

Francis Bacon

Hopes and wishes are not goals. They may kindle a fire, but they will not keep it going. Goals are tougher, more defined, and more attainable. We arrive at them by rational thought and reach them by perseverance and pluck. Our wishes may never come true; our goals are ours for the taking. The process of goal setting calls for our best, but pays full measure in return.

To be effective, to get what you want from your life and business, set goals and work persistently toward them.

a. Knowing what you want

Ours is a world where people don't know what they want and are willing to go through hell to get it.

Don Marquis

People often avoid goal setting and tumble through life quite adequately. It is a luxury that you cannot afford when starting your business. A ship doesn't leave the harbor until the captain has a destination and plots a course; neither should you. Think deeply about what you want from your business, both from a personal and a financial perspective. Do you want to work two days a week and make $200 or seven days a week and make a million? It's up to you. Just remember, you won't get anywhere if you don't know where you're going.

b. Getting support

When you have completed the goal-setting task, take time to sit down with your family and discuss what your goals will mean to them. For your family to support your goals, they must clearly understand them — both what you want to do and why. Remember that your new home business will bring changes in their lives as well as your own. Be honest. Don't try to take the easy route — false promises that the home business will exact no price from them. An already busy homemaker who starts a new business will need to take time from other tasks to run the business. A person who moves from an "away" job to a home-based job will disrupt the established routine of the household. Having support means gaining acceptance from others in the family for these changes — and countless others that will result from the new working arrangement.

If, to meet your goals, you need more consideration from your spouse or older children, be frank about it from the very beginning. If you will need more help with child care or household chores, or more respect for your working time, make sure you discuss these needs openly. While it seldom works to *demand* support for your new goals, support can be won by honesty, diplomacy, and a genuine desire to include other family members in the goal-setting process.

c. Setting your goals

One positive side effect of goal setting is that it gives you the chance to monitor your progress along the way. When you're on target, you can indulge in a little self-satisfaction. If you are not, you have time to alter course.

In Worksheet #4 below, list your goals, both personal and professional. For now, concentrate on what you wish to achieve in the first year only. Write down your goals and the interim objectives needed to reach them. Be as specific as possible.

Following a month-by-month format in this early stage will help you attain your goals and provide a checklist of your accomplishments along the way. At the end of each month, mark whether or not you reached that month's goal. If you did, sit back and gloat. If you didn't, ask yourself why, and reset the goal to the next month. Recognize that goals can at times be moving targets and that adjustments in timing may be inescapable. Just try to keep your eye fixed on your target and make whatever corrections are necessary.

Set your goals, business and personal, in order of priority. Don't set yourself up for a fall by fixing unattainable goals. Goal setting is an exercise in common sense, and objectives will be realized sooner, and easier, if they are in tandem with your time, experience, and lifestyle.

d. Commitment

You know by now that the success of your home venture will depend on you. It is your dedication, your persistence, and ultimately your commitment that provide the framework for that achievement.

Commitment is a pledge, a promise to dedicate time and resources to achieve an objective. None of us should make promises that we cannot or will not keep.

You've done a lot of work already. You've reviewed the characteristics needed for success, taken your skills inventory, set your personal and financial objectives. Take the time now to examine your ability to commit.

You can set all the goals you want, but they won't amount to a box of buttons if they are not reinforced with powerful commitment.

Commitment is permanently and inexorably attached to goal setting, and nothing can be accomplished without it. You can set all the goals you want, but they won't amount to a box of buttons if they are not reinforced with powerful commitment.

We are all imperfect beings, but some of us *think* we are more imperfect than others. We harbor nagging little fears and self doubts about our capabilities and potential. We remember every time that we failed, did not live up to our own or someone else's expectation, or fell short of success. We start, stop, step, and stumble, and every time we do, our ability to commit is weakened. Not by the quitting or missteps, but by a slow erosion of confidence.

You can rebuild that confidence, and put power in your commitment, if you focus your mental energy on your objective and move one careful step at a time. Your plans will work out and your idea for a business will expand and develop. The following suggestions will help:

- Don't talk endlessly about what you are *going* to do. Aimless discussion with friends and relatives dissipates resolve. You've no doubt heard the expression "talked to death." It does happen. Don't let it happen to your business.

Worksheet #4
Goal setting

By the end of my first year, my goal is_____

_____

_____

_____

To accomplish this:

My month 1 objective is_____

_____

_____ Accomplished?   Yes   No

My month 2 objective is_____

_____

_____ Accomplished?   Yes   No

My month 3 objective is_____

_____

_____ Accomplished?   Yes   No

My month 4 objective is_____

_____

_____ Accomplished?   Yes   No

My month 5 objective is_____

_____

_____ Accomplished?   Yes   No

My month 6 objective is_____

_____

_____ Accomplished?   Yes   No

My month 7 objective is_____

_____

_____ Accomplished?   Yes   No

My month 8 objective is_____

_____

_____ Accomplished?   Yes   No

My month 9 objective is_____

_____

_____ Accomplished?   Yes   No

My month 10 objective is_____

_____

_____ Accomplished?   Yes   No

My month 11 objective is_____

_____

_____ Accomplished?   Yes   No

My month 12 objective is_____

_____

_____ Accomplished?   Yes   No

- Test your commitment by keeping it to yourself. Formulate your business idea in your own mind and nurture it with logical, positive thinking. Let it grow for a time in quiet and solitude. Allow it to take shape slowly and carefully. As you do this, you will see your thoughts turn to resolve — and the resolve to results.

- If you are compelled to verbalize, *accomplish an objective and then talk about it.* Doing this will build true self-confidence and an independent spirit.

- When it is necessary that you talk about your plans, do so with other business people: ask for their advice, their direction, their success stories. Listen!

- Don't let the false starts of the past weigh you down. Examine them, if you will, for clues to why former ideas and projects may not have worked out — then firmly and permanently put them aside.

- Believe in yourself. It's your idea, your business. Don't listen to naysayers. Review past successes and visualize greater ones in your future.

At the heart of your enterprise is your passion to succeed. If that passion is strong enough, it will give you the personal power you need to build your dream.

For every self-confident, fearless risk taker there are a dozen quiet, persistent conservatives who achieve equal success. Both have strengths and weaknesses, but above all a powerful commitment to their goals. They have tapped their personal power. They know who they are and what they are made of. Consciously or unconsciously, they have appraised themselves, drawn honest conclusions, and forged ahead.

Every day, thousands of people start successful businesses at home. If your goals are realistic and your commitment strong, there is no reason you cannot be one of them.

WHAT THE FOOL DOES IN THE END THE WISE MAN DOES IN THE BEGINNING.

—PROVERB

4

Checking out your idea

There is the world of ideas and the world of practice.
Matthew Arnold

You are ready to begin. You are now certain that starting a home-based business is for you. You have the necessary skills and your commitment is strong. You have identified the business you wish to start and your home environment is suitable — with minor adjustments. You're confident that your service or product will be accepted by enough customers to ensure profit.

Will it?

Do you know there are enough customers out there waiting to buy electric-blue krankels, or contract for a beet-dyeing service? Can you be sure? I'm not implying that your idea for a business is frivolous. Perhaps there are customers for both ventures. What I am saying is that there is still more work to do before you risk time or money and disrupt your household. That work has a name. It's called market research.

You also want to know how competitive your market is. Will you be the only producer of krankels, or are there already a thousand of them out there? Competition is not a deterrent to going into business. Very few businesses don't face it. But it is wise to know who your competitors are and where they are so that you stand on equal ground. By identifying your competition, you can see, and learn from, what they do right and what they do wrong.

Market research is sales detective work. You do it to confirm market size and characteristics. It is an effort to minimize financial risk and save valuable time, and it points out where and how to sell

Market research is sales detective work. You do it to confirm market size and characteristics. It is an effort to minimize financial risk and save valuable time.

28

your product or service. It also tells you who your competitors are and how many of them there are. Researching your market often has an unexpected side effect of uncovering market segments that you had not originally considered.

Many start-up operations are based solely on instinct and optimism. The enthusiastic homepreneur may have only a vague idea about who the customers are or, indeed, if there will be any customers at all. Flying on blind faith, they rely on just plain old luck to see them through. And sometimes, it does just that. While every business needs a little luck now and again, banking on it is hazardous to the long-term health of your enterprise. So, if your plan is to depend on fluke or happenstance, you can skip this chapter. On the other hand, if you want to walk into your future with more certainty, read on.

Not taking the time to do some basic market research can permanently forestall success. This is the first year of your business. Why not find out now everything you can about your market? Knowing who and where your competitors are, estimating how many customers there are for your product or service, and obtaining some accurate demographics (population statistics categorized by age, income, sex, education, family size, etc.) is a credible base for your business plan.

a. Researching your market

Your market is that segment of the population that potentially may buy your product or service. Finding out who they are, and where they are, is what market research is all about. It is not as complicated as it sounds. Market research is simply the process of collecting and analyzing information. The information then forms the basis for sound decision making. It will help you pinpoint advertising, develop a marketing plan, and sell your product. Knowing your decisions are backed by knowledge and analysis not only minimizes risk, it builds confidence.

Market research seeks out two distinct types of information:

JUST THE FACTS... JUST GIVE ME THE FACTS!

29

(a) secondary data from previously published material, such as government statistics and industry reports, and

(b) primary data collected for the first time by personal visits, telephone calls, or questionnaires.

Both methods offer benefits to the start-up business.

The steps in basic market research are —

(a) Setting a time frame for completion

(b) Defining your needs (primary and secondary)

(c) Allocating resources

(d) Gathering necessary data

(e) Analyzing data

To help organize your research, use Worksheet #5 as a guide. Before you begin your project, look at each step independently and assess your own requirements.

1. Setting the time frame

Time is relevant to any business activity. As a budding home-preneur, you don't have unlimited time to pursue your research.

Decide at the beginning precisely when you intend to finish the task and work deliberately toward it. Monitor your progress as you go, and keep your original time line in view. When planning your schedule, think in terms of normal working days and eliminate weekends.

Don't allow yourself to get so caught up in research that it takes precedence over getting the business started. Remember, researching your market is a business activity; it's not *the* business.

2. Defining your need

Answer the question, "What is it that I need to know?"

If you're planning a service designed for children under 12 within a 15-block radius of your home, you need specific regional information for your area. On the other hand, if your intent is to supply a product to people over 50, by mail order, nationwide, your information needs are completely different. By properly defining your needs, you can save a lot of valuable time and avoid having to cope with information overload. Besides, there can be *too much* of a good thing. Too much data will only confuse and annoy you.

When defining your needs, decide what primary and secondary data you want.

Worksheet #5
Market research project

I will complete my market research project by: _____(mo./day/yr.)

Working days _____

INFORMATION NEEDED (In order of priority)

1._____

_____

2._____

_____

3._____

RESOURCES

Assistance required:_____

_____

Expenses:

    Postage: _____

    Telephone charges: _____

    Publications: _____

    _____   _____

    _____   _____

    _____   _____

    TOTAL   _____

SOURCES OF INFORMATION

In this section, make a list of the sources you intend to start with. List addresses and telephone numbers. Be sure to include the names of the people you contact.

Name/Address of organization	Contact name	Telephone

DATA ANALYSIS

Conclusions:

_____

_____

_____

Does the information affirm my original idea?   Yes _____   No _____

If not, what changes are indicated?

_____

_____

_____

Do the changes show a need for further research?   Yes _____   No _____

3. *Allocating your resources*

By resources I mean two things: personnel and funds. The personnel part generally poses no decision for the start-up homepreneur — you're it! But if you are starting a business with a partner or a family member, assign tasks and responsibilities and try not to get in each other's way. Perhaps one person can make phone calls while the other goes to the local library. Your research project will be more productive and efficient if you approach it in this manner. The cash required should be minimal, but undoubtedly some will be needed. Government reports and private publications may be necessary and many of them are not free.

4. *Gathering the data*

Identify and contact the most appropriate sources for the information you need. (See the next section for some places to start.) Organize and file your research results as they accumulate. Don't keep unnecessary data, and do keep an eye on your projected completion date.

5. *Analyzing the information*

Study the collected information as objectively as possible. Weigh your findings against your original idea. Does the data suggest a slight deviation from that plan? Does it affirm or negate your business premise? Cull from the data what is most pertinent to your planned product or service; date it and file it for future reference.

b. *Sources of information*

Sources of market information are many. They begin with your telephone book and end with the vast resources of the Internet. Here is just a partial list:

(a) *The Yellow Pages:* Your local telephone book can be a major resource. Before you even leave the house, study the classification that lists your competitors. How many competitors are there? Do they use display advertising.

(b) *The library:* This should probably be your first stop when you seek any business information. Helpful librarians can save you countless hours of work. Often libraries have market studies on file that can directly fit your needs. Here, you can also locate census information and trade reports.

(c) *Trade associations:* A comprehensive reference work on associations and societies is *Gale's Encyclopedia of Associations.* Check your library.

(d) *Chamber of commerce:* This is a good source for all business information. If they can't help, they will try to direct you to someone who will.

(e) *College or university business departments:* Many of these departments offer extensive research help to the new business person. Occasionally they will take on the complete market research function for a company and use it as a teaching tool for advanced students.

(f) *Government* (particularly departments for small business development): In Canada, these departments are the provinces' responsibility. In the United States, they fall under state authority. See the lists in Appendix 1 at the back of this book.

(g) *Market research companies:* These companies offer professional services, so be prepared to pay.

(h) *The Internet:* It's impossible to list all the sites on the Net that might provide you with the information you need, but as a resource it is worthwhile. If you're up to wading through the oceans of data available, go surfing (or have a Net friend do it for you). Simply engage one of the many powerful search engines using the appropriate key words and see what it comes up with. you can also check out private database companies (such as CompuServe, America Online, or Prodigy) that offer information on demographics.

c. *Methods of gathering information*

1. *Telephone*

Research for the homepreneur generally starts by picking up the telephone and asking questions. Learn to use the telephone with confidence and a winning style by following these tips:

(a) Always introduce yourself, identify your request, and ask for assistance. "My name is Joe Smith, I am planning to start a home-based business and I am looking for some information on _____. I wonder if you could help me."

(b) If the person you have reached can't help you, ask if there is someone in the department who can. If the answer is still no, ask if he or she can suggest any other department or

Facts do not cease to exist because they are ignored.

Aldous Huxley

organization. I have found this approach to be very successful and have often located sources of information that I would otherwise have overlooked.

(c) Before making any call on your research project, be sure to have your list of questions in front of you. Make certain you cover everything. Nothing is more irritating than hanging up and then remembering an important question.

(d) Make notes during the conversation, and after each call, take the time to clean up your notes, list priorities, and file the information. Remember to write down the name of the person who gave you the information; you may need to call back.

Using the telephone properly can save hours of time. It is the best possible place to start.

2. Letters

Writing letters is another useful way of gathering information. Sometimes it is a necessity because many organizations and businesses ask for requests for information in writing as a matter of policy.

To save time, it is a good idea to formulate a standard request letter. Choose a target group of organizations and government departments and do the mailing all at once. It is not absolutely necessary that such letters be typed, although I strongly suggest that they be. You are a business person, after all, and business correspondence is expected to be in a certain style and format. Typed letters have more credibility and encourage prompt action by the receiver. Your letter need not be long, but remember to state your request clearly and use a proper business format.

Sample #1 shows an example of a request for information letter from a mythical homepreneur planning a newsletter business.

3. Personal calls

In some instances, it is advisable to arrange personal meetings with people who are potential sources of information. A representative from your local chamber of commerce or the head of a trade association that could be important to your business are two examples. More than any other information-gathering activity, face-to-face meetings often lead to other important sources for data. They also establish business contacts that will be valuable in the future.

Normal business etiquette applies when arranging such meetings. Always telephone in advance to schedule a convenient time. Once again, be sure to use a winning style on the telephone. Know the name of the person you want to see and use it during your conversation. Introduce yourself and briefly indicate what you would like to talk to him or her about.

Prepare yourself for the meeting by reviewing the information you want to get. Don't waste your time, or that of the person you are meeting with, by talking overly long about your plans. Remember, you're there to learn and research. Write down information as the meeting progresses. By all means, refer to your notes and questions often to be certain that you get the information you came for.

After the meeting, once again review what you have learned, rewrite your notes, and file them.

d. The acid test for your idea

By now you have accumulated a lot of information, both first and secondhand. What is that information telling you about your idea for a business? More important, is the data leading you to think creatively about your new venture?

Now go ahead and answer the questions in Worksheet #6 below, but first, go back and reread your findings. Take a long, quiet walk, then come back and do the review.

I keep six honest serving-men (They taught me all I knew) Their names are What and Why and When And How and Where and Who.

Rudyard Kipling

October 12, 200-

Mr. James Giver
Director
Clearlake Hobby Association
Ste. 1604, 1551 Tenth Street
Marvel, Oregon 10001

Dear Mr. Giver:

I plan to publish a newsletter beginning this September. It will be issued quarterly and is targeted to people who wish to turn their hobbies into viable businesses. My research has led me to your association.

I understand that the Clearlake Hobby Association has recently completed a survey of the west coast area which has valuable detail on the "craft population" in that area. I am keenly interested in the results of that survey and would like to have a copy of it. Would this be possible? If there is a charge for it, please let me know.

I am also interested in obtaining the mailing list for your association as many of your members might well be interested in receiving my newsletter. Could you tell me the association's policy regarding sale of its membership list?

I look forward to your response. Please accept my thanks in advance for your prompt attention.

Yours truly,

Mary Jones
President

Worksheet #6
Market research

1. Is there a market for your idea?   Yes____   No____

2. Can you define who your intended customers
   are?   Yes____   No____

3. Do you know who your competitors are?   Yes____   No____

4. Can you see any advantage that your product
   has over the competition?   Yes____   No____

5. Do you know your competitor's prices?   Yes____   No____

6. Do you know where your customers are?   Yes____   No____

7. Are there enough customers to sustain
   your business?   Yes____   No____

8. Do you know how to sell your product?   Yes____   No____

9. Can you afford the selling costs of your product? Yes____   No____

10. Can you price your product competitively,
    and still make money?   Yes____   No____

Comments: The purpose of market research is to ground your plans in reality. I hope you answered a definite yes to the first 7 questions. If questions 8 through 10 still trouble you, you may not have gone far enough. Your research should help determine not only *where* you sell your product, but *how*. It will be the basis for all your sales and promotional decisions.

5

Making your business legal

A *few strong instincts, and a few plain rules.*
William Wordsworth

Rules, rules, rules. You can't avoid them, even if you do plan to operate your business at home. You might as well find out about them, comply with them, and avoid difficulties later.

North America is a large continent: 9,355,182 square miles (24,241,000 square kilometers) if you want to get specific, with the United States and Canada claiming the bulk of it, some 7,460,396 square miles (19,343,181 square kilometers) between them. Also between them they have 2 federal governments, 50 state governments, 10 provincial governments, 2 territorial governments, and I don't know how many regional and municipal authorities. They all have the power, and the strong inclination, to make laws, bylaws, rules, and regulations. Some affect you. Most, thank heaven, do not.

a. Zoning requirements

Are you legally allowed to operate your planned business from home? Only the zoning department knows for sure. *Check zoning regulations before you start your business.*

Normally, there are four types of zoning defined in local codes: agricultural, commercial, industrial, and residential. In most agricultural zones, home businesses can be operated with very few restrictions, and in commercial areas, the rule is generally to allow both commercial and residential activities. If you live in either of these zones you can expect few, if any, problems.

Chances are your home or apartment is in a standard residential area, and it is here that you will find constraints on the kind of business you can operate. The restrictions usually make sense. They are designed to protect neighborhoods from some of the more intrusive elements that can be a part of a business enterprise such as odor, noise, excess traffic, and pollution. You may find other rules that severely limit your ability to operate, such as not being allowed to sell retail, employ anyone other than family members, or store inventory.

If nature had as many laws as the State, God himself could not reign over it.

Ludwig Boerne

Many local governments already make allowances for secondary use of the home for professional people. Doctors, lawyers, dentists, and business consultants have traditionally had offices in their homes. Other countries and cities are so restrictive that they prohibit home-based businesses completely. Fortunately, such areas are the exception. If you do live in a highly restricted zone, you can ask for a zoning variance that will allow your business to operate. There is no guarantee you'll get it, but you can and should try.

In some neighborhoods, local business owners are mounting protests against home-based businesses that operate outside the existing bylaws. They are angry because such home-based establishments operate unhindered by red tape. It's inequitable, they say, when licensed, legal businesses have to abide by laws that require them to pass building inspections, have a business license, obey sign laws, and pass regular fire inspections, while home operations ignore them. They claim that non-compliance with regulations gives a home business an advantage. As a result of this protest, the zoning and licensing of home businesses is being carefully monitored in some communities. While this does not mean you can't operate your business, it does point out the need to be aware of events in your neighborhood.

Zoning laws are a municipal responsibility. To find out about zoning in your area, drop in to your local municipal offices and ask to speak to the person in charge of zoning.

For those of you who rent your homes and apartments, there is something else to consider. Many apartment owners and landlords have specific clauses in their rental or lease agreements prohibiting the use of rented space for business purposes. Now might be a good time to re-read your agreement.

b. Insurance

Discuss your business and home insurance policy with a professional. Your standard homeowner policy is not enough to meet the needs of your business. It will not cover things such as lawsuits, damages, or accidents that may result from your business. For example, suppose you have the standard homeowner policy covering you for liability. Among other things, you make Christmas decorations and once a year you have a home party to show your new products. It's snowing. A customer slips on your icy sidewalk while on her way to your party. She sues. The sole purpose of the injured party's visit was to conduct business. Will your homeowner policy cover this? There is a good chance it will not and such a lawsuit could financially cripple you.

There is a lot of fine print in the standard insurance contract that most of us don't take the time to read carefully enough. For instance, if you start a business in your home without the proper insurance, you take the chance that it will void your existing coverage. Please do not take such a risk. Be certain that you have adequate protection for your business and your home.

Some insurance companies, depending on the size and complexity of your business, will agree to add a rider to your existing coverage. A rider is an amendment to the master policy outlining and allowing for coverage beyond the standard home policy. Such a rider might list and identify your office furniture and business equipment such as computers, copiers, fax machines, etc.

Plan to discuss your business insurance needs with an agent before you start your business. A midnight burglar would be delighted to relieve you of your business equipment as it fetches top dollar in the underground market. If you keep large amounts of cash at home for the purposes of business, be sure to discuss this with your agent, too. If your business involves manufacturing a product, check on product liability coverage. This coverage protects you against lawsuits should a customer claim damages because of a defective product. While product lawsuits are most often aimed at large- and medium-sized businesses, no business is exempt. Even a nuisance suit can damage the financial health of the small home-based enterprise. While the best defense against lawsuits is a dedication to quality, customer service, and honest advertising, backup in the form of adequate insurance coverage is a sound policy.

Insurance premiums are expensive, so you should get two or three prices before you sign. The spirit of competition is as alive and well in the insurance industry as in any other and that's a good case for comparative shopping.

Reviewing your insurance is an important step in preparation for your business. Don't put it off.

c. Licenses

You must be licensed to operate a business. It is the law. What licenses you need will vary among regions and depend on the type of business you are in. In some areas, a locally obtained business license is all you need to get started. In others, federal and state or provincial licenses are required as well.

Businesses involving food handling need permits from local health departments. Check with city hall or your county clerk to see what the requirement is for your business. Your local chamber of commerce is also a source of information on permits and licenses.

The cost of a business license is minimal. The penalty for operating without a license varies with the issuing local government. If you refuse to obtain a business license, some local governments initiate court action. The result of that action can mean forced closure of your business.

d. What's in a name?

1. Register the name of your business

File and protect the name you have chosen. You can always operate your business under your proper name (e.g., Smith Electronics), but if you choose a fictitious name (e.g., The Wizard Wool Shop), or the name implies that more than one person owns the business (e.g., Smith and Company), most jurisdictions require that such names be registered. This is done by filing a "fictitious name statement" with county or provincial authorities. When you register a fictitious name, it will be checked against previously filed names to ensure the name has not been taken by another business. This is for your protection, too. Once your name is on file, it cannot be used by anyone else.

Many people start their businesses and do not register the name. This can be a costly mistake. You may operate for a few months or longer, all the while spending time and money to get your company name recognized and respected, then one day you receive a registered letter in the mail telling you to stop using it. Too late, you find out that the name is already used and protected by someone else. You may even be liable for damages.

It is a good idea to have two, or even three, names ready before you register. That way, if your first choice is rejected you have another name ready, and you don't have to start all over again. A quick — though not foolproof — way to check the availability of the name is to scan your local telephone book.

In Canada, you can have a name search done through the provincial ministry that handles incorporations. This will also tell you if the name is registered out of province. This process takes about a week and there is a small fee, generally under $50.

In the United States, your city or county clerk will tell you if the name you have chosen is available for use.

Don't order expensive stationery and business cards before "saving" your name: you could end up out of pocket. You can always use your whole personal name — Meg Spears, Interior Design, for example. But if you are using only part of your name — for instance, John's Gardening — you should register it.

2. *Choose a suitable name*

Choosing the right name for your business is important, and there are things you should consider.

(a) The name should reflect the business you are in. Try to let the name of your company tell the customer a little about what your company is about. If you are operating a word processing service, for example, you might call yourself Wordworks or Quickwords.

(b) The name should not mimic large, well-known companies. Even if your name is Henry Ford, it wouldn't be wise to call your home-based auto repair service, Henry Ford Automotive Service. It might get a chuckle or two, but chances are your customers simply would not take the business seriously.

(c) The name should not limit your business to one activity. If you start out making pies and call your business Jane's Pies or Only Pies, you should plan on making pies forever. The name will be a drawback if you decide to sell cream puffs or the world's best brownies. Try something more generic like Oven Wonders or Gourmet Bakers.

(d) The name should lend itself to creative advertising and promotion. Try to visualize the name in advertising copy. Come up with a strong tag line that fits with the name. If you're in the lawn maintenance business, for example, you might be called Elegant Lawns: A cut above the rest.

(e) The name should be easily spelled and spoken. Avoid multi-syllable words in the name. Keep it concise; it will be more easily remembered. A company named Triederwastonberg Party Services will soon be forgotten. It's simply too much work to remember.

(f) The name should be lasting, not "faddy." Your name is the most visible sign of your business. It should stand the test of time. If, for example, you started your home-based hair salon a few years ago and called it Afro Cutters, the name would now be dated and obsolete. On the other hand, if you had called it Great Hair, the name would be just as good today as it was then. Use a tag line if you want to specialize.

e. Sales tax permits

You will require a sales tax number if your business buys goods for resale. This regulation applies in all provinces and states that have a sales tax. You will be collecting tax from the buyer of your product and that tax must be remitted to the tax office with the tax number.

In the United States, contact your state tax office, describe the nature of your business, and ask for the appropriate permit. The rules and procedures for remitting the tax will come in the mail with your permit. Failure to collect and remit such tax is a serious breach of tax law.

In Canada, contact the provincial tax department to obtain your tax number.

Note: In Canada businesses are obliged to collect and remit the goods and services tax (GST), which is a tax on virtually all goods manufactured and services provided in Canada for use in Canada. There are very few businesses exempt from this tax, but if your annual revenue is less than $30,000, you may fall under the "small trader" section of the legislation and be one of them. Your local Revenue Canada office will provide details on the tax and the filing requirements. Check the blue pages of your phone book. (At the time of writing, the Atlantic provinces had merged their provincial sales tax with the GST into the "harmonized sales tax," or HST. Contact your local tax offices for latest details.)

f. Start-up information sources

There is an almost unlimited supply of information available to anyone planning to start a business. Some is specific to home-based business and some is more general. All of it is worthwhile, most of it is free, and it is as near as your telephone. I suggest that you take the time now to gather as much of this information as you can. It will form a solid base of reference material as you move from the planning stage of your home-based business to full operation.

I strongly encourage you to take full advantage of these information services. At this stage in your planning process, you just can't make any better use of your time. Information is dynamic; it changes constantly, so keep in touch with your local Small Business Administration (SBA) office, or in Canada, your local office of the Canada Business Centre. Don't be timid about asking questions about any of the programs or regulations that you don't understand. Remember the old adage, the only truly stupid question is the one you don't ask.

1. In the United States

In the United States, the Small Business Administration (SBA) offers a wide variety of publications covering topics such as budgeting, market research, legal structure, marketing, and financing. The SBA also offers literature specific to the home-based business such as *How to Start a Home-Based Business* and *The Business Plan for Home-Based Business*. Here's how to contact them:

- Call your local SBA office — there are offices in every major city — and ask for a small business counselor.

DIDN'T I SUGGEST WE SEEK PROFESSIONAL LEGAL AND ACCOUNTING ADVICE? AND WHO SAID, "OH NO, WE DON'T NEED A GUIDE"?

- Call the SBA's Small Business Answer Desk toll-free at 1-800-ASK-SBA (1-800-827-5722).

- Access the SBA Web site at *http://www.sbaonline.sba.gov*. For an overview of what SBA has to offer, its Web site really delivers.

Also available as a resource through the SBA is SCORE, the Service Corps of Retired Executives. If you require counseling of a specific nature, you may be able to find a volunteer through SCORE who has direct experience in your business.

2. *In Canada*

A good source for business information in Canada is your Canadian Business Service Centre (CBSC). These centres are a collaborative effort by the federal and provincial governments and the private sector. They offer information on business-helpful government programs, services, and regulations, a fax-back service to get the information to you quickly, and a library of videos, publications, directories, and CD-ROMs geared to business.

To contact your centre, check your phone book. Every provincial CBSC has its own toll-free number. You will find their Web site at *http://reliant.ic.gc.ca*. Another Web site worth investigating is Strategis, created by the federal government to provide current information on government programs, policies, and regulations. You'll find it at *http://strategis.ic.gc.ca*.

Also contact the Business Development Bank of Canada (BDC). The BDC excels in facilitating seminars and workshops for the entry-level business person at a reasonable cost. Many of the seminars are conducted in non-urban areas and many are industry specific. The BDC also provides a variety of publications that will make good additions to your reference library. *Preparing a Business Plan* and *Credit and Collection Tips* are just a couple of examples.

The Canadian Business Development Bank also offers a Business Management Support Program (BMS) consisting of a roster of qualified counselors prepared to work with you on a one-on-one basis. Such counseling covers start-up and beyond. BMS is offered nationwide and the charge for this expertise is minimal.

If you do not have a BDC office near you, call its toll-free number: 1-888-INFO-BDC. You can access its extensive Web page at *http://www.bdc.ca* for more complete data.

g. *Your legal structure*

The homepreneur, like any good business person, should choose the business structure most suitable for his or her enterprise. The question is, do you wish to function as a corporate or noncorporate entity?

The noncorporate forms of business include sole proprietorship, general partnership, and limited partnership. General and limited partnerships are the noncorporate forms for businesses with more than one owner. The difference between the two is that the partners in a general partnership have unlimited liability while the limited partners may limit their liability to the amount they have invested.

Of the noncorporate forms, sole proprietorship is the one often used by people setting up their home businesses. It is the simplest and least expensive way to start out. The corporate form is another option. While it may cost more initially, it could be right for you depending on the nature of your enterprise.

Note: There are tax advantages and disadvantages in each of the possible business structures, and incorporation is governed by state or provincial laws. You should obtain legal and tax advice before making your final decision.

1. *Sole proprietorship*

This is the simplest method of setting up a business. Many businesses start this way and incorporate later. The sole proprietorship and the owner are one entity in the eyes of the tax department.

Advantages:

- You avoid incorporation costs at the outset.
- You may have a lower rate of taxation.
- Business losses can sometimes be used to offset other income. (This must be checked with an accountant.)

Disadvantages:

- You are personally liable for all your business debts.
- Some government loans or guarantee programs are not available to the sole proprietor.
- It can be difficult to raise capital.

2. Corporation

When you form an incorporated company, you create a separate and distinct entity. The corporation has a life of its own; it is the corporation that is taxed, assumes debt, sues, and is sued.

Advantages:

- Limited liability. You are not personally responsible for the corporation's debt.
- The corporation is easily sold.
- Often it is easier to raise money.
- A corporation is perceived as having more status.
- Possibility of lower tax rate.

Disadvantages:

- There is a cost to incorporate.
- There are more government regulations to comply with.

Note: The limited liability aspect of incorporated companies is often of little value to the start-up business person as most professional lenders will require a personal guarantee when you borrow money.

As you can see, there are pros and cons to each structure. In making your decision, consider taxation levels, regulations, and commercial law as it affects your business. Professional advice from an accountant and lawyer will prove helpful in your decision-making process. Remember, it is possible to start your business as a proprietorship and incorporate it later when the business warrants it.

h. Professional services

If you read a lot of books about starting a business, and I hope you do, you will find conflicting opinions on when you should hire a lawyer or accountant. The reason for the differing advice is rooted in cost. No one trying to guide a new business through the start-up period wants the business owner to spend more money than he or she has to. This counsel is well-meaning, but the time will come when the new business needs professional advice on matters of law or accounting.

Accounting and law are highly specialized areas, and each is subject to constant change. It is difficult for the homepreneur to keep up with these changes and still run a profitable business.

Although professional advice is expensive, it is often necessary to avoid costly mistakes. If you are unsure of legalities that affect your business or are confused about proper accounting procedures, you should use the services of a qualified accountant and lawyer.

The legal and accounting professions exist because of a definite need in the marketplace. A lawyer is invaluable if you are sued, need advice on business law, are required to sign a contract, or enter into a partnership agreement. A good accountant can guide you through the labyrinth of tax regulations and in doing so save you hundreds, perhaps thousands, of dollars over the years of your business. Tax reform in both the United States and Canada has made the services of a professional accountant a necessity for even the smallest business enterprise.

It is wise to plan for your professional services early in your business cycle, to take the time to select who you want to act for your new business, and to check credentials. The other option is to wait until you have a problem. This method can be perilous. If your mind is occupied with a problem, it is not always clear enough to choose an adviser wisely. If the problem is serious and you are under stress, you may even engage the wrong person entirely and spend more time and money than you need to. It is better to establish a comfortable working relationship from the beginning. You do not need to pay a king's ransom for professional services if you prepare yourself and your business properly.

i. Choosing your lawyer

The best way of finding a lawyer is through referral. If you have friends in business, ask them who they use and if they are pleased with the services provided. Your banker is also a good source for a recommendation. Remember that lawyers specialize. One might have developed a talent for tax, another, insurance claims, and yet another might put effort into labor law. A friend who refers you to the lawyer that handled her marriage breakup is doing you no favor. You want someone whose specialty is corporate law, not divorce proceedings.

In your search for a lawyer, you can also use the Yellow Pages. You will notice that most of the lawyers indicate their professional specialty and many offer a free initial meeting. Before making an appointment to meet, try to have a brief telephone conversation. Enquire about rates and the lawyer's speciality. Tell him or her a little

The sharp employ the sharp; verily, a man may be known by his lawyer.

about your business and gauge the level of interest expressed. If the conversation goes well, ask for a meeting. At this point, remember you are seeking a lawyer, not advice, so be sure your intentions are made clear. Your preliminary meeting with any lawyer should be free. Be certain this is understood before you make your appointment. In fairness to the lawyer, keep the meeting brief. Time is the professional's stock-in-trade, so don't waste it.

Selecting your lawyer is an important business decision. If you are starting from scratch with no referrals to help you out, it's a good idea to talk to at least three lawyers before making your final decision. Make sure the lawyer you choose has experience with small business. If he or she does work for other home-based enterprises, that's even better.

A good lawyer will not do all the talking. He or she will be interested and ask questions about your business. If this is not the case, regard it as a warning signal and say a quick goodbye. It is essential that your potential legal counsel show a genuine desire to learn about your enterprise.

Look for a lawyer who has the ability to communicate. You should never leave your lawyer's office without a complete understanding of the problem or issue you have discussed. Unfortunately, many otherwise excellent lawyers do not have good communication skills. They persist in speaking legalese when talking about even the most mundane aspects of the law. Choose a lawyer who speaks your language. You have a right to understand completely the advice you pay for.

A conscientious lawyer is a great asset to your business, so take the time to choose wisely. He or she will be an integral part of your business for many years, and it is essential that the relationship have a high degree of trust. Don't wait until you are beset by problems and in an emotional turmoil to make your selection.

Don't rely on your lawyer to make decisions that will affect your business. Lawyers are not business people. They are paid to give advice, not to draw conclusions. That is, and will always be, your responsibility as the business owner. When faced with a legal dilemma, by all means consult your lawyer. If you get a clear understanding of the governing law, an assessment of your liabilities, and some sound legal advice, your lawyer's job is done. The rest is up to you.

Once you have selected your lawyer, take steps to keep legal costs in line. Remember: lawyers bill for time. As soon as you meet, the clock starts ticking. Each tick means more money for his or her business and less for yours, so it pays to be a clock watcher and set yourself a few rules:

(a) Be prepared. When you have a problem and need legal advice, think it through in advance. Be able to describe it thoroughly and succinctly when you meet your lawyer.

(b) Make lists. Write your questions down and take them with you. Being organized saves time.

(c) Don't socialize while the clock is ticking. While you should maintain a cordial relationship with your lawyer, remember that you are paying for every minute of that discussion of the weather, the family pet, and last night's football game.

(d) Stick to the facts. Your lawyer and your pocketbook will be best served if you keep to the matter at hand. Don't ramble away from the issue. Know what you are there for and stay with it.

(e) Avoid unnecessary phone calls. A lawyer bills for advice given over the phone the same as for a personal visit. Don't call without a reason.

(f) Get documents in order. If your visit is necessary because of contract negotiations or partnership problems, review the information before the meeting and have the right paperwork at hand.

j. Bookkeeper or accountant?

There is a difference between bookkeepers and accountants. Generally speaking, an accountant is a certified professional with years of experience and specialized training. A competent bookkeeper is a professional with years of experience. Many bookkeepers also take special training while others have learned strictly by doing.

1. The professional accountant

Those initials behind the professional accountant's name mark him or her as a qualified and often very expensive professional. Accountants not only prepare financial statements and tax returns, they can also set up a bookkeeping system, prepare budgets, and provide general financial advice on everything from insurance planning to lease-versus-purchase decisions. And if you need tax advice, it is a professional accountant you go to, not a bookkeeper.

51

As a home-based business person you do not need to become a tax expert, but basic knowledge is essential to the financial health of your venture.

In Canada, there are three different designations that a professional accountant might use: C.A. (chartered accountant), C.G.A. (certified general accountant), and C.M.A. (certified management accountant).

In the United States, look for the designation C.P.A. (certified public accountant).

The primary reason for using the services of a professional accountant is to avoid undue taxation. With so many recent tax changes in both the United States and Canada, the preparation of tax returns has become something of an ordeal for all but the most intrepid souls. If you are not one of them, plan to engage a qualified professional. He or she is your best line of defense against undue taxation.

If you are completely unfamiliar with taxation and its possible effect on your new business, set up an appointment with an accountant and seek some general tax advice. Ask him or her what you can do to minimize the tax paid by your new venture. Be aware of tax and its effect on your enterprise from the beginning. As a home-based business person you do not need to become a tax expert, but basic knowledge is essential to the financial health of your venture.

An accountant can also assist you in setting up a set of ledgers to record sales and expenditures that is both useful for your particular business and consistent with accepted accounting principles.

Use the same good sense in selecting your accountant as you do when you choose your lawyer. If you can get a referral, great. If not, go through the same process as you did to find a lawyer. Again, make certain that the accountant you pick can communicate clearly. Jargon from the world of finance can be just as confusing as legalese. Hourly rates for a professional accountant vary, so make sure you understand the billing method.

Many of the homepreneurs I have spoken to visit their accountant only once a year — at tax time. While most of them are confident of their ability to keep an accurate and up-to-date set of records, few feel as sure about their skill in matching wits with the tax collector. They minimize the costs of using an accountant by presenting him or her with organized, well-kept records at year end.

To keep your professional accounting charges in line, follow their lead. If you present your accountant with a shoe box stuffed with miscellaneous, unsorted receipts and checks, you can expect him or her to charge a shoe box full of cash.

2. *The bookkeeper*

Accounting — the preparation of financial statements, tax returns, and so on — takes considerable skill and special expertise. Bookkeeping — keeping track of sales and expenditures and entering them in a ledger — does not. You can and should do your own bookkeeping in the early stages of your business. By doing so, you learn the numbers that make your business tick.

On a day-to-day basis, the business owner is making one decision after another, and most of them have a financial side effect. Singly, such decisions seem small, perhaps even insignificant, but taken as a whole they create a total picture of your business and its financial well-being.

By sitting down at least once a month and systematically entering the transactions you have undertaken, you are reminded of the cause and effect of your business decisions. Doing your own bookkeeping not only helps you understand the financial underpinnings of your business, it will help you communicate more effectively with your accountant when tax time rolls around. You may not choose to do the bookkeeping for your company forever, but in the start-up period it is a sensible route to take. (For more information, see *Basic Accounting for the Small Business*, another title in the Self-Counsel Series.)

As your home business prospers, you may decide your time is better spent on sales and management activities. That is the time to hire the services of a bookkeeper. Once again, try to get a recommendation from a business associate. Alternatively, check the classified ads in your local newspaper or the Yellow Pages. Many bookkeepers are home based, so look for one near you to save traveling time. The hourly rates of bookkeepers vary so be sure to comparison shop. Most are well below the $100 and up hourly charge of a professional accountant.

You can keep the bill from your bookkeeper to a minimum if your paperwork is properly organized when you submit it. If you have been doing your own books up until now, you will have no difficulty in selecting a bookkeeper and outlining the exact services you require.

k. *Hiring employees*

If you must hire employees in your first year of business, there are still more rules and regulations to contend with. There are laws governing minimum wages, hours of work, and health and safety concerns, just to name a few. You must withhold and remit the employees' tax, unemployment insurance/social security, and, in most cases, workers' compensation funds. You are also obliged to prepare paychecks for the employees and year-end payroll tax returns for the government. The administration demands create a paperwork burden that most new homepreneurs find much too time consuming. If you wish to avoid it, there are alternatives:

(a) **Work with other home-based businesses**

If you do word processing, for example, seek out colleagues with similar expertise and set up a working arrangement where they will handle overload projects. This may cut into your profits on occasion, but if your need is small, it may prove less costly than hiring staff.

(b) **Use temporary placement agencies**

Personnel agencies will supply you with staff on an as-needed basis. They can send people who will work for a few hours (most have a minimum of four) or a few weeks. When the job is done, the agency bills you for the time by invoice. They take care of all necessary deductions and reporting for that employee. The hourly charge for using an agency may be higher than you would pay an employee, but it will save you paperwork.

(c) **Use contract staff**

This is similar in concept to using an agency in that the contractor submits an invoice at the end of the job. He or she accepts responsibility for paying taxes and prepares whatever reports are necessary to maintain contract status. Because contractors do not have the overhead of a personnel agency, they are often able to bill you at a lower rate. You cannot, however, simply hire an employee and treat him or her as a contractor. The tax department doesn't permit it. You are probably on safe ground if the contract person you hire provides services to more than one client and keeps a set of books for his or her services. It is also a good idea to have a written document that clearly outlines that the arrangement is indeed a contractual one.

In both Canada and the United States, the tax departments reserve the right to define when a person is a contractor or an employee, and in both countries year-end reports are required. There are special forms designed to cover non-employee compensation. In the United States, if the amount is over $600, Form 1099 is needed. To be certain, contact the Internal Revenue Service (IRS). If you are hiring employees, ask for Circular E, Employers' Tax Guide. It outlines the rules, regulations, and deductions required.

In Canada, if the amount is over $500 (or if you have withheld tax for the contractor), you must submit Form T4A. Contact Revenue Canada if you have questions. You can also ask for the form Employee/Employer Relationships if you wish to set up a contract arrangement. For information on rules, regulations, and deductions for employees, Revenue Canada has a useful guide: *The Employer's Kit.*

Publications from both the IRS and Revenue Canada are free, and both the IRS and Revenue Canada have large Web sites. In some cases you can download the forms you need. For the United States, go to *http://www.ustreas.gov* and for Canada, *http://www.revcan.ca.*

6

Start the forecasting habit

Habit is habit, and not to be flung out of the window by any man, but coaxed downstairs a step at a time.

Mark Twain

People starting new businesses often reject the idea of forecasting or financial planning. "I'm no psychic," you might say. "How can I possibly predict what will happen a year from now or six months from now, for that matter." You're absolutely right; you can't — not with perfect certainty. What you can do is estimate, and based on your knowledge and research, you can greatly increase your chances of success and eliminate some unpleasant surprises. Forecasting sales and expenses may prove a challenge in the beginning when you have no financial history to help you out, but it can and should be done.

Business risk, at home or elsewhere, should always be *calculated* risk, and you can calculate that risk from the very beginning. Once you start the forecasting habit, it is hard to break. The exercise of forecasting makes such a contribution to the health of your business that you'll find yourself doing it every year. Like any exercise, with practice, it gets easier and easier.

In past years, a certain mystique has surrounded the business and financial forecasting process. Some people think that it takes professionals with special knowledge or a finely honed set of skills. There may be truth in that if your plan involves forming a multi-national corporation or risking millions to tap into the Japanese market. But your goal is not quite so grand. You have two common sense issues

You have two common-sense issues in mind as you start your home venture: you want to know what the costs are and what you can expect to earn.

56

in mind as you start your home venture: you want to know what the costs (risks) are and what you can expect to earn (profit) from your new business. To do this, you must think carefully and logically about what you aim to do.

a. Some good reasons to forecast

Forecasting may be compared to a slightly near-sighted man putting on glasses for the first time. His new glasses don't give him X-ray vision or enable him to spot a hurricane a thousand miles away, but they do improve his ability to see and respond to his immediate environment. That is what forecasting will do for your home business. So what are some good reasons to forecast sales and expenses for your new enterprise?

A well thought out forecast will —

(a) indicate the funds required for your business. Do you have enough money or will you need a loan? This question must be answered early if you are to avoid financial woes during the start-up period of your venture.

(b) prove or disprove the feasibility of your idea. There is nothing like the objectivity of a few numbers to tell the truth, the whole truth, and nothing but the truth. Some business ideas do not pass this test, and it's better to know early in the business cycle before making a financial commitment.

(c) encourage you to think about factors critical to your business such as costs, equipment, space needs, etc. You will have some essential demands and expenses in your business. A detailed examination of all aspects of the business helps you to avoid unpleasant surprises.

(d) allow you to "see" your business on paper before you spend large sums of cash. This is an excellent exercise. Not only does it point out the possible downside, it also shows the financial potential of your enterprise. A vision of your success, supported by solid calculations, is a great aid to motivation and planning.

(e) indicate at what point your venture will break even and then show a profit. In the first few months of most businesses, the cash out exceeds the cash in. Having some idea of when this cash tide will turn in your favor encourages financial planning — personal and business.

(f) help a potential lender judge the merits of your business. You have to do a forecast if you approach a lender for money. It's an important ingredient in a lender's decision-making process. An accurate forecast allows the lender to understand your business and see clearly how borrowed money will be repaid.

(g) prepare you for the risks inherent in starting your home-based business. Stress and worry about business is often rooted in the unknown. I'll say it again. Business risk should always be calculated risk. If you prepare for the risk, you can approach it without fear; if you don't, you're in for a bumpy ride.

(h) tell you how long your start-up funds will last. Whether you begin your business with $100 or $100,000, you will want to estimate how long that initial pool of money will last. The most important question to be answered in a forecast is "Will my start-up capital last until sales contribute cash to my business?"

Any one of the above is a good enough reason to forecast your sales and expenses for the first year of your business. There are others. Forecasting develops your skill as a homepreneur and business person by encouraging you to be both realistic and sensible in your approach. It gives credibility to your concept and helps you to base your decisions on fact, not fancy.

b. What you need to know to forecast

Forecasting can be as simple or complex as you want to make it. Let's try it the simple way, with no complications and just one slow step at a time.

A good forecast is based on as much fact and as little fiction as possible. This means that you must first analyze your existing resources — things such as cash on hand, equipment, etc., and then project what you can earn by using those resources wisely. To do your forecast, you must *know* the following:

(a) Your cash investment: How much cash on hand do you have to put into your new venture? Cash on hand is the first entry for your cash flow forecast. Whether it is $50 or $1 million, it is an absolute.

(b) Loans or outside funds: If you are using money from an outside source, how much is it? Is it a loan or a direct investment from a partner?

(c) Your business capacity: How much of your product or service can you produce, taking into consideration time and equipment available?

(d) The price you will charge for your goods: Your price ultimately creates your sales figure. How much will you bill for your product or service?

(e) The cost to produce your product or service: There will be costs that relate directly to the production of your goods. What are they?

You must also sensibly *predict:*

(a) The amount of goods or services you will sell: Here you must gauge your sales effort and market acceptance for your product and place them in a logical time frame.

(b) All the expenses of running your business: Advertising, telephone, furniture, and office supplies are a few examples. You must estimate what these expenses will be and when you will have to write checks to pay for them. A little homework on what things cost can go a long way to creating a realistic expense forecast.

As you move through this chapter, you will have an opportunity to review each of the above. By the end of it, you will have prepared a cash flow forecast for your new business.

c. *Cash flow or operating statement forecast?*

The most important forecast for a new business is cash flow. It differs from an operating statement or operating forecast because it deals only with the flow of cash in and out of the business. Cash receipts and cash payments are estimated and allocated to the month in which they occur. By creating a cash flow forecast, you paint a picture of cash movement through the business, both coming in and going out. You might compare it to the ocean's tide. The tide is high when the water (cash) comes to shore. It is low when it goes out. The difference is that cash flow in a business is not quite so predictable, particularly in year one.

An important reason to be aware of your business tide is to help you plan major purchases and expenditures at the right time. You won't make the mistake of buying that new computer or taking a bonus at the wrong time if you know in advance your cash is going out rather than coming in.

The operating statement forecast shows sales and expenses too. However, it shows the month a sale is billed, not the month the cash is received. It shows expenses when they are incurred, not the month the check is written. It also does not show the cash invested by the owner, loan proceeds, or investment from other sources.

The reason I suggest that you concentrate on the cash flow forecast is that the operating statement forecast does not show if there will be enough cash on hand to meet the needs of the business. For someone starting a new business, having a firm understanding of cash flow in and out of his or her business is a necessity.

d. Planning your cash flow forecast

Thinking is where planning begins. At the end of this chapter, we're going to take the results of that thinking and put it on paper in the form of a basic cash flow forecast for the first year. Such a forecast is just one part of a full business plan. There are others if you intend to raise funds from outside sources; they are summarized in chapter 7. For now, let's just concentrate on forecasting your cash needs for year one and covering some important items that should be considered before you begin the forecasting process.

Along with loans and personal investment, the cash flow into your business is created by sales of the product or service your business offers. The amount of cash your business will earn will depend on the rate at which the product or service will sell and the price you charge. Understanding the cash needed to produce the product or service and pricing correctly is a large part of cash flow planning.

The goal of business can be reduced to one simple objective: to bring in more cash than goes out.

The cash flow out of your business is the result of the costs of producing your product or service and the expenses of administering and managing the business. The goal of business can be reduced to one simple objective: to bring in more cash than goes out. To plan and monitor that process you develop a cash flow forecast.

e. *What price will you charge?*

Pricing is tied to marketing. What you charge your customer has a direct effect on your potential sales. Finding and charging the right price is critical to your sales effort and your profits. If your price is too high, you meet with price resistance and the customer won't buy your product. If your price is too low, the customer might assume the goods are cheap or shoddily made and refuse to buy for that reason. Striking a balance and making a profit is the challenge.

There is nothing more demoralizing than a small but adequate income.

Edmund Wilson

Consider these factors:

(a) How much does it cost you? After considering all the costs necessary to produce your product or service, make sure you have enough markup to ensure your own profit. If you are buying a product for resale, rather than making it, you know exactly what it costs — the price you pay the manufacturer.

(b) How sensitive is your market? The price of your product should be readily accepted by your intended customers. If your product is expensive by nature, your target market should not be in the lower income bracket. Remember, if you price your product too high, it will result in lost sales and maybe no sales at all.

(c) What image do you wish your home-based business to project? If you plan to target the low-income sector with your service, you won't need embossed letterhead and gilt-edged business cards. Inexpensive flyers can replace glossy brochures. You will want your image as well as your price to represent economy and quality.

SUPER SUCCESSFUL SALES PEOPLE EXPECT SUCCESSFUL RESULTS.

—DAN KENNEDY

(d) What does your competition charge? You can't ignore what is perceived as the going rate for a product or service unless you can prove and sell that your product offers a definite advantage.

f. Pricing strategies

Many pricing strategies work. Many successful companies use more than one. Listed below is a small sampling.

1. Cost pricing

Cost pricing is the cost of the product plus a percentage markup. Example: Your product costs you $8.50 to make. After considering the sensitivity of your market, product image, and the competition's price, you decide that a 30% profit over those costs is reasonable. You mark up the product that amount and charge your customer $11.05.

$8.50	X	30%	=	$2.55
cost price	X	*markup overhead*	=	*profit before*

$2.55	+	$8.50	=	$11.05
profit before overhead	+	*cost price to customer*	=	*selling price*

2. Discount pricing

Promotions, coupons, and sales are examples of discount pricing. Discount pricing is often used to introduce a new product or service. It is most often used when sales volume is expected to be high.

3. Market penetration pricing

Market penetration pricing is consistent low pricing in order to gain a larger share of the market. This type of pricing is often used when the seller has "deep pockets" — the financial strength to withstand losses on a product until it has a recognized position in the market.

4. Competition pricing

Competition pricing is setting prices based on what the competition is charging. Competition prices should be a guide, but this system of pricing can be risky if you do not completely understand your costs and expenses. What if your competition has those deep pockets mentioned above?

Effective and profitable pricing decisions should be thought out carefully and tuned to your selling strategy. For the start-up homepreneur, cost pricing is a sensible choice, but you should also consider what your customer will pay and what your competitors are charging. Your market research should have given you some insight into both factors. Be flexible when necessary and develop a system to monitor your pricing practices on a regular basis. Costs, competition, and markets change; keep a sharp eye on each of them as your business grows.

g. *Costing your product*

Before setting your price, be sure just what your costs are. Using 10 units (products) as your base, calculate the cost of the labor and materials required to produce that number. Worksheet #7 will help you with these calculations. (Note that 10 is an arbitrary number. If it is more effective for you to calculate by 12 or 100, adjust the form accordingly.)

h. *Pricing a service*

The driving force behind pricing in your service business is what you need or want to earn as an hourly rate. If your enterprise is competitive, the limitation is what your competitors charge for a similar service. If the going rate for word processing in your city is $20 an hour, for example, there's not much point in trying to charge $50 an hour.

In a fee-for-services business, your hourly rate should take three things into consideration: labor, overhead, and profit. The calculation is simple: labor + overhead + profit = price.

For example, suppose you want to make $20,000 per year from your home service business. As you will be billing your customers on an hourly basis, you must arrive at your hourly wage rate. You must decide how many days you will work and how many hours in that day will be billable. There are 365 days in a year. You plan on one month's holiday per year so knock off 31 days, leaving 334. Exclude remaining weekends and you have 238 working days. You plan on 6 billable hours per day. Take 6 times 238 for a total of 1,428 billable hours per year. Dividing $20,000 by 1,428 tells you that you must clear $14 per hour to make your desired income. To ensure that you clear $14, you must bill enough to cover overhead expenses and profit.

The most common mistakes made by home-based service business owners are undercharging and making no allowance for the overhead or fixed expenses of running their business. They establish

Worksheet #7
Costing your product

COST TO MAKE 10 UNITS

MATERIAL:

Material description	Quantity	Cost	Amount
_____	_____	_____	_____
_____	_____	_____	_____
_____	_____	_____	_____
_____	_____	_____	_____
_____	_____	_____	_____

TOTAL FOR MATERIAL $_____

LABOR:

Activity	Hours	Rate	Amount
_____	_____	_____	_____
_____	_____	_____	_____
_____	_____	_____	_____
_____	_____	_____	_____
_____	_____	_____	_____

TOTAL FOR LABOR $_____

ADD TOTAL LABOR & MATERIALS =   _____

DIVIDE BY 10 =   _____ EACH a rate of pay for themselves and do not consider the telephone costs, additional electricity, insurance, or other expenses entailed in running the business. Worse, if they hire an employee, they often make no profit at all!

If your idea is to run a service business at home, do not undervalue it. Think carefully about all the costs associated with the service and charge accordingly. If you primarily sell time, be sure to keep time sheets. If you give fixed prices for work performed (e.g., per page keying price, flat rate for cleaning 9 x 12 carpets, etc.), time sheets will provide good documentation and allow you to analyze your productivity and profit. If you do employ others, make sure you include fringe benefits in your hourly cost. Such things as unemployment insurance or social security and workers' compensation add substantially to your labor costs. Also monitor and include costs for supplies associated with your service and allow for wastage.

Maintain accurate and detailed time sheets and itemize all your activities on behalf of a customer. Many service companies are plagued by disputes about bills that do not outline exactly what the charges are for. You invite such disputes if you send out bills with general wording such as, "Services rendered: $300." Be specific.

i. Indirect costs and overhead

Labor and materials are not the only costs associated with your business. They represent the direct costs only. Direct costs are linked to your product or service and vary depending on sales volume. There are indirect costs as well; these are costs over and above direct costs and are appropriately called overheads. Payment for indirect, overhead costs must also show in your cash flow forecast. Overhead costs include things such as insurance, electricity, telephone, and other general expenses incurred as a result of running a business. They are also called fixed expenses, meaning that the expense will be constant whether you make 10,000 krankels or none, work 10 hours or 100. You cannot avoid incurring some fixed expenses when you start your business. It is best if you keep them to a minimum until your business has matured and you are more confident about the expenses your business must carry as "permanent" expenses.

It is in the area of fixed expenses that the homepreneur makes the greatest savings, most particularly by not paying rent for outside office or production space. But you will have some overhead beyond your product or service cost, and it should be considered before you set your price. We'll deal with some possible fixed expenses later in this chapter.

j. *Marketing costs*

1. *What is marketing?*

Marketing is critical. It is one thing to design and build a product, or to have an idea for a needed service, but it is quite another to gain acceptance for it in a busy, oversold world.

Many people confuse the terms "marketing" and "sales." Are they the same thing or aren't they? Both are concerned with getting the goods into the customers' hands, but there is a difference. Marketing is the more comprehensive term. It *includes* sales, but also involves all aspects of creating and increasing demand for a product or service, research, pricing, advertising, and distribution.

You can see by that definition that you, the homepreneur, are a marketer. Marketing is a critical and fascinating challenge, and it is elemental to the business process. It is one thing to design and build a product, or to have an idea for a needed service, but it is quite another to gain acceptance for it in a busy, oversold world.

2. *Cost considerations*

What follows are some methods used to sell products and services. Think about each of them as they may relate to your marketing plan.

(a) Advertising: Will you be using newspapers, trade magazines, professional journals, or classifieds? If so, how much do such ads cost? How many times will you run them?

(b) Direct sales: Do you have plans to hire a full-time salesperson? Will you be paying salary or straight commission?

(c) Promotion: Are you planning home demonstrations or special product promotions? Will such events require special brochures? What about free samples or other sales aids, such as pens with your company name on them, etc.?

(d) Mail: Will you be using the postal service as a means of selling? Do you plan on buying a mailing list? Have you considered the cost of postage? Printing? Art work?

As you can see, regardless of the method you choose to sell your product or service, there is a cost associated with it. Sales and marketing require cash. Marketing costs must be estimated and allocated to the month in which payment is due. If you hire a salesperson, enter the salary or commission as a sales expense for the months in which it will be paid.

Worksheet #8 will help you begin to think about some of the other costs associated with your marketing plan.

To make your information more accurate, gather data from local sources. For example, if you plan to advertise, contact local publications, newspapers, etc. for their advertising rates. If you are planning to create a brochure, talk to a local printer to get some idea about art and printing costs. A couple of phone calls will give you some practical input for your budget.

k. Other overhead costs

Now you are almost ready to develop a cash flow forecast for your business. Before you do, review those overhead costs talked about earlier and make a list. Fill in Worksheet #9 and stroke out any items that do not apply to your business and add any that are missing. Think of all expenses that might occur in your business on a regular basis. Exclude costs directly related to your product or service such as material and labor. Beside each item on the list, put down the cost and then show if the expense is paid monthly, quarterly, or yearly.

l. Start-up costs

Other variable costs to consider when you do your first forecast are start-up costs. Start-up costs for the homepreneur might include things such as new office furniture, equipment, or initial inventory. If you sign a lease for equipment of any kind, you might have to make a first and last month payment. All such expenses should be documented and considered in your cash flow forecast. Think of any one-time, start-up costs you will incur for your business.

In Worksheet #10, list the start-up costs that might be required for your business and allocate them to the month that the money is due.

m. Forecasting your first year's sales

By now you have a working knowledge of what it will cost to produce your product or provide your service and a good grasp of your monthly expenses. It's time to forecast your sales. Take a few minutes and go back to your market research materials; do a short review of the information. Remember that you want your budget

Worksheet #8
Estimating marketing costs

HOW?	WHEN?	HOW MUCH?

Advertising:

_____ _____ _____

_____ _____ _____

_____ _____ _____

_____ _____ _____

Promotions:

_____ _____ _____

_____ _____ _____

_____ _____ _____

_____ _____ _____

Direct mail:

_____ _____ _____

_____ _____ _____

_____ _____ _____

_____ _____ _____

Other:

_____ _____ _____

_____ _____ _____

_____ _____ _____

_____ _____ _____

Worksheet #9
Indirect costs and overhead

ITEM	AMOUNT	HOW PAID		
		Mo.	Qrt.	Yr.
Telephone	_____	____	____	____
Automobile	_____	____	____	____
Deliveries	_____	____	____	____
Insurance	_____	____	____	____
Utilities	_____	____	____	____
Dues and memberships	_____	____	____	____
Licenses	_____	____	____	____
Office supplies & expenses	_____	____	____	____
Travel	_____	____	____	____
Accounting & legal	_____	____	____	____
Health plan	_____	____	____	____
Equipment rental	_____	____	____	____
Wages & benefits	_____	____	____	____
Interest & bank charges	_____	____	____	____

Worksheet #10
Start-up costs

Description of purchase	Amount	Month
_____	_____	_____
_____	_____	_____
_____	_____	_____
_____	_____	_____
_____	_____	_____
_____	_____	_____
_____	_____	_____
_____	_____	_____
_____	_____	_____
_____	_____	_____
_____	_____	_____
_____	_____	_____
_____	_____	_____
_____	_____	_____
_____	_____	_____
_____	_____	_____
_____	_____	_____

and sales forecast to be as accurate and realistic as possible. You want a sensible, practical model of year one.

Forecasting sales for a new business is one of the most difficult steps in preparing your cash flow projections. The good news is that it becomes less so after you have been in operation a year or so and your sales have established a pattern. Don't expect perfection in your first forecast. If you review your research, consider seasonal impact, and give the best estimate you can of the results you expect from your own efforts, it will be a good start. You can fine-tune your sales projections as you gain a greater knowledge of your market.

The first question the homepreneur must answer before projecting a sales figure is: "What is my capacity to produce?" Capacity is fundamental to estimating sales. It takes into account the space available, labor, equipment, materials, and financial resources of the business. Capacity is what you can do, not what you want to do. There is little sense in forecasting sales of 50,000 krankels if you can produce only 2,000, or in projecting 4,000 hours of billable time if you plan on working only four months of the year.

For the first-time forecaster, knowing and relating sales to capacity helps to simplify projecting a sales figure. It also helps to schedule and organize the business. What is the capacity of your home-based business? Think in terms of a small unit of time and work your way up. How much of your product or service can you produce for sale in the following periods?

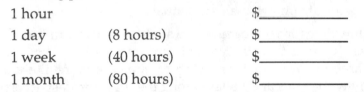

1 hour		$_____
1 day	(8 hours)	$_____
1 week	(40 hours)	$_____
1 month	(80 hours)	$_____

The method of calculating capacity shown above creates the *ideal or theoretical* capacity. If you apply the price of your product or hourly billing rate to this maximum capacity, please remember that you have created an *ideal or theoretical* sales figure. This is not the sales figure that you wish to show on your forecast! All this figure will do is tell you what, in the best possible circumstances, your business might produce.

The theoretical figure is fun to dream about, but such pie in the sky is hard to attain and even harder to maintain.

Very few businesses ever operate to full capacity on a continuing basis. They have periods when staff is short, equipment fails, or sales demand falters. Proper sales forecasting always takes these events into consideration. Let's normalize your capacity before we go any further. Apply some common sense to your new organization and redo the chart.

How much of your product or service will you produce for sale *under normal operating conditions* in a good month?

1 hour		$_____
1 day	(____ hours)	$_____
1 week	(____ hours)	$_____
1 month	(____ hours)	$_____

Barring the purchase of additional equipment or added labor to increase your capacity, the figures you entered above should show the maximum sales attainable in your new business. Applying realistic production numbers to the price of your product gives you a good idea of what to expect from your business. It also helps you to avoid extravagant and unreasonable sales projections.

n. *Projecting your sales trend*

You know what you could bill out in the best of all possible worlds. Now, give some thought to other factors that will affect your sales figures in the first year. As you try to project a plausible growth curve, include any events, planned or otherwise, that will contribute to or detract from your sales potential.

Allow time for your business and sales to grow. I'm sure there are some businesses that start with maximum sales from day one — but they are rare. Your sales and cash receipts are more likely to grow slowly with peaks and valleys along the way; forecast accordingly.

Consider what influence the seasons have on your enterprise. Will December be better than March? Will the back-to-school season create business or will this be a slow time? If your product or service sales ebb and flow between spring and winter, so will your cash. Seasonal impact should be reflected in your cash-flow planning.

On Worksheet #11, do a quick graph of your first year in business. *Don't think about actual sales numbers.* You're not ready for that. Think instead about the *events and influences* that will shape your business in its first 12 months. Remember to include things such as planned vacations, family responsibilities, the time it will take you to build sales, seasonal influences, special promotions, and when you can expect results from advertising or your own sales efforts.

Assign month names under the row of zeros starting with the first month of your business. Then think carefully about what kind of month each will be for your enterprise. Using the numbers on the worksheet, circle ten if you think that month will be an excellent month for cash into your business. Circle a one if you think the month will be poor and zero if you expect no cash at all. When you are finished, join the circles with a line to see the sales trend you are predicting for your business.

Doing this exercise will help your thinking process when you begin to assign projected sales figures to your cash and expense forecast. At the bottom of the worksheet, make notes to yourself on why a month is expected to be high or low in cash receipts.

o. *Review of cash flow forecast requirements*

Before starting your cash flow forecast, ask yourself the following questions:

    (a) Have I arrived at a price for my product or service?

    (b) Is my product or service priced to sell?

    (c) Have I considered my pricing strategy?

    (d) Have I established the costs of my product?

    (e) Do I know what my overheads (indirect costs) are?

    (f) Have I planned how to market my service or product?

    (g) Do I know the costs associated with my marketing plan?

    (h) Have I established my start-up costs?

    (i) Do I know my "capacity" to produce my service or product?

    (j) Have I considered a plausible growth curve?

    (k) Do I know what impact, if any, seasonal changes will have on my business?

    (l) Have I decided how much of my own cash I will invest?

It is a bad plan that admits of no modification.

Publilius Syrus

If you have considered all these questions and applied your best judgment to each of them, you have the ingredients for your first cash flow estimates. You have done exactly what Mark Twain suggested at the beginning of this chapter "coaxed it downstairs, one step at a time." All that needs to be done now is some simple arithmetic.

Worksheet #11
Projected sales trend — year one

```
      10   10   10   10   10   10   10   10   10   10   10   10
       9    9    9    9    9    9    9    9    9    9    9    9
       8    8    8    8    8    8    8    8    8    8    8    8
       7    7    7    7    7    7    7    7    7    7    7    7
       6    6    6    6    6    6    6    6    6    6    6    6
       5    5    5    5    5    5    5    5    5    5    5    5
       4    4    4    4    4    4    4    4    4    4    4    4
       3    3    3    3    3    3    3    3    3    3    3    3
       2    2    2    2    2    2    2    2    2    2    2    2
       1    1    1    1    1    1    1    1    1    1    1    1
       0    0    0    0    0    0    0    0    0    0    0    0
```

Month: ___ ___ ___ ___ ___ ___ ___ ___ ___ ___ ___ ___

Month 1:_____

Month 2:_____

Month 3:_____

Month 4:_____

Month 5:_____

Month 6:_____

Month 7:_____

Month 8:_____

Month 9:_____

Month 10:_____

Month 11:_____

Month 12:_____

p. Sample cash flow forecast

As you have probably guessed by now, I am in the business of making electric blue krankels. (There seemed to be just too much competition in the widget business.) Sample #2 shows a cash flow forecast for my first three months of business with an explanation for each entry.

I thought about my activities and expenditures carefully before I did my forecast. I have never been a mathematical genius, but I did want to know how long my cash would hold out. A cash flow forecast was the only way to do it. I considered the items in the forecast one at a time, did my best to appraise seasonal impact and personal commitments, made lists — and plunged in. What follows are some of the decisions and assumptions I made for the first three months of the Electric Blue Krankel Company. (See Sample #2 to cross-reference numbered notes.)

1. The selling price of a krankel is $6. I established the costs of my materials and planned my initial inventory accordingly.

2. I predicted how many krankels I would sell in the first three months. On the first line of my forecast I put the number for products sold for cash and on the second line the number for credit sales. This wasn't necessary, but it helped me to re-member my capacity and made the cash flow a more visual exercise.

3. I entered my cash sales in the cash receipts section of my forecast. (Number of products sold for cash x my price of $6.)

4. I listed my credit sales, allowing a time lag for receipt of payment. My terms are 30 days from date of invoice, so I don't expect any money from credit sales in Month 1 and I entered zero. In Month 2, I estimated that I would collect about 50% of Month 1 credit sales (10 x $6), and in Month 3, I projected that I would collect the balance of Month 1 credit sales (10 x $6) and 50% of Month 2 (20 x $6) for a total of $180.

5. I listed the money I had borrowed from the bank ($2,000) and my personal investment ($3,000).

6. I totalled my cash receipts (Cash in).

7. I thought about all my expenses and when I would have to write checks to pay for them. I paid particular attention to Month 1 because of start-up costs. Among other things, I had to prepay for some inventory, buy some office furniture, get

Sample #2
Cash flow forecast for first three months

Electric Blue Krankel Company

	Month 1	Month 2	Month 3
① Product sold @ $6.00 each			
② For cash	50	75	100
On credit	20	40	45
Cash receipts			
③ Cash from sales	300	450	600
④ Cash from receivables	0	60	180
⑤ Loan proceeds	2,000		
Personal investment	3,000		
⑥ Total cash receipts	5,300	510	780
⑦ Disbursements			
Inventory purchase	500	200	200
Wages		500	500
Licenses	75		
Utilities	75	75	75
Furniture	500		
Advertising	500		200
Car expense	100	100	100
Bank charges	25	25	25
Loan repayment		75	75
Insurance	150		
Equipment rental	75	75	75
Telephone	80	80	80
Printing	125		
Miscellaneous	100	100	100
⑧ Total disbursements	2,305	1,230	1,430
⑨ Cash surplus (Shortage)	2,995	⑬ (720)	(650)
⑩ Cash on hand			
Beginning of month	⑪	⑭ 2,995	2,275
End of month	⑫ 2,995	2,275	1,625

some printing done, and pay the first installment on my insurance. I also decided to do some advertising.

8. I totalled my disbursements (Cash out).

9. I subtracted my disbursements from my cash receipts to find out if I had a surplus or shortage of cash at the end of the month.

10. At the bottom of my forecast, I calculated the cash on hand.

11. For the first month of my business, it wasn't necessary to show a beginning-of-month total in the cash on hand section; it was the same as the number shown in the cash receipts section at the top of my forecast. Cash on hand for Month 1 is the money I started with.

12. My first end-of-month cash figure is simply the difference between my cash receipts (Cash in) and disbursements (Cash out). I have almost $3,000 left for the coming month's expenses.

13. I calculated my Month 2 cash surplus (shortage) in the same way as the first, estimating my product sales, cash receipts, disbursements, etc. There weren't nearly as many expenses as in Month 1, but because the only money coming into the business was from sales, I do end the month with more cash going out than coming in. I have a cash shortage.

14. To calculate my end-of-month cash on hand for Month 2, I had to have a beginning-of-month balance. Easy. I just took the end-of-month cash figure from Month 1 and moved it to the beginning-of-month cash section for Month 2. After I did that, I subtracted my cash (shortage) to give me a new end-of-month total for cash on hand.

The most important asset your business has — besides you, of course — is cash, and the most important number in your forecast is the one that shows the cash on hand at the end of each month. When it shows a negative balance, you know that you do not have enough money to meet your obligations for the coming month.

q. Doing your forecast

All you need to begin your forecasting process is a block of uninterrupted time, your notes, a calculator, a 13-column pad, and a pencil. If you have a computer with spreadsheet software, you can skip the pad, pencil, and calculator.

The computer spreadsheet is a remarkable time-saving tool for cash flow forecasting and many other business planning activities. It not only simplifies the procedure by doing all your calculations, but also allows you to make changes easily and quickly. Dedicated business planners and forecasters convert quickly to using computer spreadsheets.

A spreadsheet program is the computer version of the column pad. It is an electronic worksheet composed of rows and columns that interact with each other at the touch of a key. Once you have entered the information, it is easily changed, updated, and recalculated.

If you are a computer user now, you will have no difficulty adjusting to this method of planning. I seriously doubt you would consider developing your forecast in any other way. If you are not a computer user, see if you can find a friend who has a spreadsheet program and is willing to show you how it works.

If the idea of using technology makes you nervous, start now to overcome it. Few businesses at home or anywhere else can afford to ignore technology and the benefits it offers. Working with a "user-friendly" spreadsheet program is as good a place to start as any.

Whether you use a computer or a pencil, you will follow the same format for your cash flow forecast as I used for my Electric Blue Krankel Company. Your forecast should, of course, cover at least the first 12 months of your business.

r. Cash planning

The importance of your cash flow forecast cannot be overstated. To consider starting your home-based business without one is foolhardy in the extreme.

Managing your cash is a continuing process. Your forecast is only the beginning. Once you begin billing your customers and collecting receivables, there will be an even greater need to become adept at cash planning and control. (You will find some tips on caring for your cash later in the book.) If you do not control your cash, you won't control your business, and chances are you will lurch from one financial crisis to another. Be good to yourself and your new venture; start planning for your cash needs from the very beginning and continue to do so over the life of your enterprise.

The cash flow within your business is dynamic; it changes constantly. Consequently, your forecast cannot be a static document. It requires frequent updating. Plan now to set aside time for cash planning on a monthly basis. Compare your forecast to the realities of your business and make the necessary adjustments. Become attuned to the trends of your business and the influences that affect it. If you do this, the task of forecasting will be easier and the results more exact as your skill increases.

Although this chapter has concentrated on the cash forecast for the first 12 months, you can and should project further than the first year as soon as possible. When you are more at ease with the cash planning process, begin forecasting for year two, three, and beyond. Successful business people always know when and how financial commitments will be met. Forecast, and plan to be one of them.

7

Raising the money

Money is like a sixth sense without which you cannot make a complete use of the other five.

Somerset Maugham

Starting and running a home-based business takes money. It may require less than its rent-paying cousin in that downtown highrise, but it needs cash just the same. Without sufficient capital, a business can quickly become tiresome and stressful. Enthusiasm and motivation both suffer when there is no money in the bank account to meet next month's bills or finance those new orders. You might compare it to starting out early in the week with a light cold, nothing serious. But it turns mean with the first sign of damp weather. By Friday, you have pneumonia. To ward off a case of pneumonia in your business, be certain you have enough capital to start your business.

The cash required for your venture can come from a variety of sources: your personal savings, relatives and friends, banks, private investors, and, sometimes, the government. Most business funding is a combination of the above. Review each option as discussed in this chapter and think about which ones will work for your business.

However, before you think about borrowing money, from whatever source, keep in mind the risks involved. Most people have a debt tolerance level. That tolerance is higher for some small business people than for others. They will borrow against their personal and business assets to the maximum, and it appears to cause them no discomfort or worry. They live their business lives without a financial safety net and appear happy doing so. To such people, owing a lot of money is almost a status symbol. It's as if they say, "Look at me. I must be successful. Look at all the money I owe." This is not a wise way to run a business.

As a business person, you should always feel a little uneasy about debt and work hard to keep it under control. Understand and be aware of the damage that irresponsible borrowing can have on a business. Unnecessary debt cripples a business, eliminates options, and weakens its ability to survive. You may not be able to escape it entirely as your home-based business grows and prospers, but if you must borrow, *borrow only what you need and only when you need it.* By following this simple rule, you ensure two things: a stronger business and a calm state of mind.

a. Personal savings

If you have enough personal resources to run your business until it yields a profit, you are home free. It is a powerful way to start out. You have no anxious lenders to account to and no financial responsibilities other than to yourself and your business — and no bank interest to pay. There is no better, or less stressful, way to start a new enterprise than debt free.

If the financial demands of your business are small, consider waiting, and saving, until you *can* independently fund your enterprise. Two out of three homepreneurs I spoke to about start-up capital recommended this as the best way to start.

b. Relatives and friends

Money provided by relatives and friends is called "love money." Most often, love money takes the form of a loan. The money is lent on trust, accepted with good intentions, and no collateral is required. Many home enterprises begin with the generosity of loved ones.

If the business is successful, and the money is repaid promptly, both parties remain happy and satisfied. There are good feelings all around. If not, the borrowed money can become a contentious issue that survives much longer than the ill-fated enterprise. There is always a danger in mixing money with a personal relationship, well-meaning as it might be, and it is wise to consider carefully before asking for such a loan. If love money is a financial option open to you,

Some people use one half their ingenuity to get into debt and the other half to avoid paying it.

George D. Prentice

give the possible consequences serious thought. Is your business worth the risk of a friend or family member's money?

If you do start your enterprise on love money, it will no doubt be your intention to pay it back through the profits of the business. Your cash flow forecast will help you determine if this is a reasonable plan. Before agreeing to the loan, think about a backup payment plan should the business be unable to repay the debt.

The terms and conditions of the loan should be fair and negotiated in a businesslike manner. Be scrupulous in honoring the trust that is inherent in such a loan. Prepare a proper promissory note that outlines all the terms and conditions. (Promissory note forms can be purchased at most stationery stores.) Most important, be as certain as you can of your ability to pay it back on time and in full.

c. Banks

1. The business loan

Most business operators still use the banking system to borrow money. Surveys show that 80% to 90% of businesses use the bank as their main resource for cash. In theory, the homepreneur should have no more difficulty getting a business loan than any other business person. Your good sense in planning to operate your business at home to keep expenses down should even give you a slight edge. In fact the reverse is true.

It is often more difficult for the home-based business person to negotiate a business loan than his or her downtown office counterpart. One reason is image. The homepreneur is often not taken seriously as a committed business person. Another reason is poor presentation. Remember, a banker must qualify you and your business as credit worthy. To do this, he or she needs accurate information that shows your expertise and commitment to the enterprise. Take the time to develop a business plan and package the loan request in a complete and professional manner. If your business idea is sound, and you do your homework, you should not have a difficult time.

2. Establishing the right borrowing image

Home-based business has its roots in the idea of someone wanting to make "a little extra cash." Historically, it was a sideline activity of the spouse not employed outside the home. He or she worked at the "business" when there was time to do so. They seldom *made* time for it, and it was secondary to just about everything else that went on in their lives.

Personal hobbies formed the basis for many such businesses. They were often called "hobby businesses." The "business" was never intended to grow very much or take precedence over the earnings of the main family supporter. It was enough that the hobby pay for itself and provide that little extra cash. Many such businesses operate today. They live up to the owner's expectations by providing personal satisfaction and some financial support for a labor of love. Bookkeeping is minimal, many times non-existent, and real profits, if any, are seldom calculated. Such businesses don't have to worry about impressing the local bank manager.

It is the image that *all* home businesses are similarly hobby based, that they have limited commercial potential, and that they are not a priority for their owners that lingers in the minds of professional lenders. This preconceived notion can hamper the serious person who is trying to raise funds for a home-based venture.

Before writing this chapter, I spoke to a number of bankers who work in the small business area. All were aware of the growth in home-based enterprise. All were helpful. Now might just be the time to pass some of their comments along.

I wanted to know if there was any foundation to the image problem. I asked: "Is there any difference between someone coming in to seek funds for a home-based business versus any other kind of business?" Their replies were consistently "No," but most added qualifiers. They said they took into account how small the businesses were and how new they were, and pointed out that they had to be concerned that there was no *real* track record for what one banker referred to as "the home-based business industry." (Personally, I am heartened by the use of the term "industry." It's clear that home-based business is now recognized as a viable and credible commercial endeavor.)

When you're starting a home-based business, you can't avoid being new or small, and that there is no track record isn't your problem. However, it is wise to understand that it is a problem for the banker. It puts a greater onus on you to prove your worth and the worth of your business.

I also asked how the home-based business person compares with other business people in presenting their case for a loan. Here are some verbatim responses:

"Overall? Badly."

"They're totally uneducated."

"They don't put enough effort into planning."

One of the bankers, perhaps with tongue in cheek, replied, "They make me work too hard. I like the questions answered before I ask." She, too, was referring to the lack of business information provided by the would-be homepreneur.

Such criticisms can be dealt with. The image of your home-based business is easily enhanced by just doing a little research and preparation. Plan to do better than expected, to be professional, to be informed. Answer the banker's questions before he or she asks and you'll increase your chance for a business loan. *Most important of all, prepare a basic business plan before approaching any banker for a loan.* (See section **f.** in this chapter.)

3. *Understanding your banker*

When you approach the bank for a business loan, your head will probably be full of what you want, what you need, and what you must have to get your enterprise up and running.

While this is natural and necessary, it does make you forget that a loan involves two partners, the borrower and the lender. The lender approaches the loan from a completely different perspective than that of the borrower. To avoid unrealistic expectations, keep this in mind. An understanding of the other person's point of view is the basis of successful negotiating.

Think about it. You know where you're coming from and what you can and can't do to secure your start-up funds. What about the banker? He or she has limitations and constraints as well which include established bank regulations and personal ambitions. It is these very constraints that often lead to an adversarial relationship between banks and business people. You may not agree with them, but you cannot ignore them. Here are some things that you should know about banks and bankers at the outset:

(a) The bank will not assume total responsibility for financing your business. If you expect to start and run your business using only the bank's money and none of your own, you're in for an unpleasant surprise. They expect you to have enough faith in your business to invest your money, too. One of the first things they will look for is the dollar amount that represents your financial commitment.

(b) Banks require that you have enough collateral to cover the funds borrowed. I've heard some wild stories about people who borrow from a bank without security or collateral of any kind. To my knowledge, that's just what they are — wild stories.

   The banker is bound by his or her responsibility to the bank to ensure that any loans made are as secure as possible. Collateral can be your home, cash, bonds, or other negotiable securities that can be claimed should you default on the loan.

(c) Banks expect you to have a strong commitment to your business. While this commitment often takes the form of your personal cash, it also includes your dedication to researching your business and your continuing good judgment in the running of the business.

(d) Your local banker doesn't make the rules. He or she is bound by the policies and regulations that affect the bank as a whole. Your banker probably has a loan limit that can be granted without authorization from head office or an immediate superior. Beyond that limit, it's out of his or her hands.

(e) It is not in your banker's interest to make a "bad" loan. Bankers are people too, remember, and they are judged by the amount of successful business they do. They want to be judged well. They function within a corporate structure that demands performance if they are to advance. The desire to avoid making bad loans often makes a banker ultra conservative.

(f) Some banks and bankers are better than others. It pays to do some research before you approach any bank for a loan. Ask for information before you ask for money. Try to understand how the bank works. Is it aggressive in its pursuit of new business? Is there any special data that they want on your business before being asked for financing?

(g) Banks do not do business on a handshake. They require documentation on your plans for your business. The evaluation of your business and the decision to grant a loan is a serious task for your banker. Records must be kept and information must be properly prepared. A nice friendly chat just won't cut it.

4. *Personal financing options*

Many of the homepreneurs that I have spoken to found that taking out a personal loan was the most direct route to cash for their

The banker is bound by his or her responsibility to the bank to ensure that any loans made are as secure as possible.

business. They simply borrowed the funds they needed under their own names. While they still needed to have sufficient collateral to cover the loan, they did not have to advise the banker on all details of their business venture. Later, as their business and its ability to pay off debt increased, they switched to commercial borrowing. This type of loan is generally term financing: money received in a lump sum with a specified pay-back period that includes payment on the amount borrowed plus interest.

Taking out a personal loan is sometimes the easiest method for many home-based businesses, particularly when the amount needed for start-up is small. There is no requirement for a business plan and in some instances the cost of the money can be less. As long as you have the collateral and can satisfy the bank of your ability to pay, you should have no more difficulty obtaining this type of loan than if you were purchasing a new car. If you plan on this type of borrowing, be sure to incorporate the principal and interest payments in your cash flow forecast. Remember that the money is for your business, and it will go into your business records as a loan from you. You borrow from the bank and your business borrows from you.

If you have a long-standing relationship with your banker and good collateral, you may be eligible for a personal line of credit based on your credit rating and ability to pay back the loan. A line of credit gives you the opportunity to borrow money as needed up to a specified limit. It may provide you with the flexible financing you need to begin your operation. The only way to discover your personal borrowing capacity is to talk to your banker. You can do this with no obligation on your part.

Some home-based businesses start by using the unused line of credit available to them on their credit cards. Some credit cards have lines of up to $10,000 available. It is often overlooked as a source of business cash. One banker I spoke to recommended this as a quick alternative to bank financing if the loan amount is small. *Use caution if you use credit card financing to start your business.* This kind of money is expensive! I don't recommend credit card financing if other, less expensive money, can be had through other banking methods.

If you are asking for a personal loan or line of credit and you are married, the bank will probably require the signature of your spouse. The reason for this is that often the collateral for the debt is in both names. *It should not be necessary for both spouses to sign if there is sufficient security solely owned by the borrowing spouse and he or she can clearly demonstrate ability to pay.*

Before granting a personal loan or line of credit, your banker may ask you to provide a statement of personal worth. He or she will probably give you a form designed by the bank for this purpose. A statement of personal worth is a snapshot of your financial health: a list of what you own (assets) and what you owe (liabilities). The difference between the two represents your financial worth.

Sample #3 shows a typical statement of personal worth form. Particular banks may require more or less information depending on their needs. If you are married, and the assets and liabilities are in both your names, information on both spouses will be required.

d. Private investors

A private investor can be hard to find. Many people trying to start a business look for investors by taking out a classified ad in their local newspapers. I think it is obvious that this approach is risky. Going into business with someone you know can be difficult: with someone you don't know, it can be impossible. Be very careful if you choose this approach. Should you find an investor in this manner, check him or her out carefully. Ask a lot of questions. Don't let your good sense evaporate because a stranger is willing to put cash on the table. This is one time when you *should* look a gift horse in the mouth.

Money obtained in this way generally comes with conditions. The investor may want control of the company, for example, or, if the money takes the form of a loan, an extremely high interest rate. While such conditions can be fair depending on the degree of risk, often the strings attached to this kind of financing can be so stringent as to limit your ability to control your operation effectively.

A better source for finding private investors is your accountant. People with money to invest in small, start-up ventures often rely on their accountants to guide them. They will ask the accountant to keep an eye out for promising business investments. If your accountant happens to be the potential investor's accountant, a good relationship can result. Expect such investors to be cautious and to attach conditions to the loan. Their approach to lending money or taking an equity position in a small business is similar to that of a bank. They require complete and accurate information on the business seeking funds. They will seldom invest in a home-based business unless there is a possibility of a greater-than-average return on investment.

Sample #3
Statement of personal worth

Name:_____   Date:_____

Address:_____

_____

Telephone: _____

Employers:

Present:_____   How long?_____

_____   Position:_____

Previous:_____   How long?_____

_____   Position:_____

Current salary:_____   Other income:_____

ASSETS			LIABILITIES	
	Amount			Amount
Cash on hand	_____		Loans	_____
Stocks & bonds	_____			_____
Life insurance	_____		Charge accounts	_____
Home	_____		Mortgage	_____
Automobile	_____		Other	_____
TOTAL	_____		TOTAL	_____
NET WORTH: (Assets - Liabilities)				_____

e. Government

The governments of both the United States and Canada provide some financial assistance to small business.

In the United States, funding is administered through the Small Business Administration (SBA). The reason for SBA's existence is to help small business, and while the majority of this help is educational, some financial assistance also exists.

Anyone thinking about a home-based business should make themselves aware of the SBA's Microloan Program. This program deals with *very* small loans — as low as $100. The maximum available through this program is $25,000. It works like this: the SBA provides funds to non-profit intermediaries who qualify, then loan to eligible borrowers. The loans, when properly documented, can be processed within a couple of weeks. Terms can be as long as six years, depending on the business's earnings. Such loans do, of course, require collateral and, in most cases, the borrower's personal guarantee. Check your local SBA office or call the SBA Small Business Answer Desk at 1-800-827-5722 (1-800-ASK-SBA).

In Canada, money for small business comes through a variety of government departments, both federal and provincial. The best source for information is your nearest Canada Business Service Centre (CBSC). They can advise you on government programs, what type of business qualifies, and where to apply.

The Business Development Bank of Canada (BDC) is also a possible funding source. The bank offers a Micro-Business Program aimed at small business. Loans as low as $5,000 are available for business start-up, acquisition of fixed assets, and, in some cases, market surveys and product research. For more information, call your local BDC or call their toll-free number: 1-800-INFO-BDC.

"AND YOU HAVE A REASONABLE EXPECTATION OF PROFIT IN BUSINESS AS A SELF-EMPLOYED HULA-HOOP INSTRUCTOR?"

It should be noted here that most government lending, in both the United States and Canada, is done as "last resort" lending. It often takes the form of loan guarantees rather than direct loans. Government is not, nor should it be, in the business of competing with banks, trust companies, or other commercial lending institutions. You will probably be required to prove that you were unable to obtain money from other sources before approaching government for money. Generally, they will expect that you have some of your own money invested in the enterprise.

Before approaching any government lending department for funds, prepare proper documentation on your business. The rules of preparation and professionalism apply any time you seek either commercial or government financial assistance.

Many government programs give loans to or guarantee loans for incorporated businesses only. Small proprietorships often find themselves ineligible for certain types of government funding. Even if you do strike out, the process of learning what is available through the various levels of government is worthwhile. You may not be eligible now, but there may be a time later in your business cycle that your business will qualify, and the time spent will not have been wasted.

f. A business plan for your banker

Your business plan should be pragmatic enough to encourage trust and prepared well enough to sustain interest.

Your business plan should be a simple, honest document that describes your experience, your business, and your plans for its future. It need not be long or complicated, but it should tell a complete story in a way that can be easily understood by a potential lender. It is also a sales document developed to present your business in a positive way. It should be pragmatic enough to encourage trust and prepared well enough to sustain interest.

While your business plan is expected to follow a certain format, it can be tailored to suit the situation. The banker does not expect you to submit 100 pages of data if you are seeking a small loan. The bankers I spoke to said they would welcome three or four pages of solid information and a cash flow forecast. So we'll concentrate on the basics.

He fishes well who uses a golden hook.

Latin proverb

1. The substance

The following factors are the essentials of a business plan required for a loan application. If you have thought carefully about your home-based business and its financial needs, you should have no difficulty putting the necessary data on paper. Don't let the process intimidate you. Keep your presentation brief and make every word count.

(a) Summary

In the traditional business plan, this section is called the Executive Summary. It outlines the background and history of the business, states the company objectives, says how much money the business requires, and shows clearly how and when the business will repay the funds. You should follow the same pattern. Your business doesn't have a history yet, but you should outline the essentials of the proposed business: what it does, location, legal structure (proprietorship or incorporated company), names of any other shareholders, the amount of funds required, and terms under which the money will be repaid.

(b) Experience and background

This section should contain your résumé and those of any other key people involved in the business. Emphasize why your experience and that of your partner or key person is valuable to the business. Make sure the lender understands that you have the background and experience to run the business. This is a critical part of your presentation. Lenders look favorably on loan applications that give a strong indication of the applicant's ability to "make it happen." They are very aware that mismanagement is one of the main causes of business failure.

(c) Description of product or service

Describe your product or service clearly and concisely. Explain why it is necessary and why it will do well in the chosen market. Emphasize any advantages that your product has over its competitors. If it is unique in any way, highlight that. Use this section to feature the benefits your business realizes by being operated from your home. Does operating from home allow you to sell your product or service at a lower price? If this is the case, say so.

To help you get started, here is a sample statement. Let's assume you are a designer and manufacturer of scarves. Your description of your product might read something like the following. Remember, it need not be a lengthy statement, but it should be clear.

> *XYZ Company designs and produces "pre-fashioned" scarves for boutiques and specialty stores in the state of Oregon. While scarves have always maintained a place as a fashion accessory, recently they have become more popular than ever.*

The attractiveness of scarves rests in the ability of the wearer to shape and tie them properly. Many wearers admit to a certain lack of creativity when it comes to highlighting a favorite outfit with the addition of a scarf. With its unique cutting and tying method, XYZ Company eliminates the need to tie or shape the scarf. The XYZ scarf is an instant fashion accessory, and its distinctive design gives it a special place in the fashion accessory market. (A picture is still worth a thousand words — if a good photo will help your cause, include one.)

The inventory required to produce the scarf, mainly high-quality silks and specialty fabric, requires little space. Equipment space requirements are also minimal. It is for this reason that the business is operated from the home. As a home-based enterprise, the business foregoes costly rent payments, therefore enabling it to use its capital for the expansion of the business.

(d) Selling strategy

Provide details on who your customers are and how you intend to reach them. In this section, it is wise to show that you have done your market research and that you are using that research as the basis of sales strategy. If your product or service is a competitive one, describe the competition. Experienced lenders are very aware that many new business ventures often don't succeed because of poor marketing and sales planning. They will expect you to have a good understanding of the market you have chosen to operate in.

(e) Cash flow forecast

Your cash flow forecast should be a truthful projection of the sales and cash needs of your new home-based business. It should tell the banker that the business has the ability to pay back the amount borrowed. *Don't present your banker or potential lender with overly optimistic forecasts; they cannot be fooled!* If there is one mistake new business people make, it is presenting unrealistic forecasts. You might as well try to pass a $3 bill.

Anyone who even considers lending money wants a business plan grounded in reality and common sense. If you have been going through this book step by step, you have already done your cash flow forecast. Go over it again. Try to develop a fresh perspective and view the plan from a lender's point of view. Most lenders will automatically look for the downside of your plan — the worst case. (If you've got a genuine talent for business, so should you.) Prepare yourself and your plan for scrutiny; be ready for any questions that may be put to you.

(f) **Statement of personal worth**

Bankers will normally request a personal worth statement when a loan applicant has no prior history with the bank. While you may not choose to present this statement with your business loan application package, you might save some time by having a current one tucked in your briefcase. Pick one up at the bank before your visit or prepare one similar to Sample #3 shown earlier.

2. *The form*

How your plan looks is important to your loan application. It should be clean and crisp. Use standard size paper, black type, and double space all copy. There should be no typos, spelling mistakes, or grammatical errors. If you are uncertain about your language skills, have someone proofread it. It should have a separate cover page that contains the company name, address, telephone number, and your name as the person to contact for further information. It should also show the date the document was prepared.

You might consider writing a courteous covering letter asking the bank to consider the enclosed documentation and offering to provide any additional information that might be required. If you choose to write a covering letter, make sure the person's name and title are correct.

Each section of the plan should have a heading and the pages should be numbered.

The SBA in the United States has several publications available to help you develop your business plan. Ask for Publication MP 11, *Business Plan for Small Service Firms* and MP 15, *The Business Plan for Home-based Business.* These publications cost $1 each and are approximately 20 pages long.

The Business Development Bank of Canada offers the *Business Planning Package, Do-It-Yourself Kit.* The kit is designed in worksheet-style modules and covers such topics as arranging financing, forecasting and cash flow budgeting, analyzing financial statements, evaluating the purchase of a small business, and credit and collection tips.

Also check the information circulars available at major banks. Many banks provide helpful publications on financing and business planning.

For detailed, step-by-step advice, you might wish to read another title in the Self-Counsel Series, *Preparing a Successful Business Plan.*

g. *Check your attitude*

Any new business person's first foray into the financial community often engenders a feeling of awe. The experience may make you nervous or uneasy. After all, none of us is a creature of resolute self-assurance all the time. What confidence we do have has a way of abandoning us at the most inopportune moments.

More than anything else in the world, we fear rejection, and certainly when we first ask for a loan, rejection is a possibility. The carefully worked out business plan and the wonderful profit-making ideas seem inadequate as we approach the first lender's door. There he or she sits, looking splendid behind an imitation oak desk, and there we are with our plan, ink barely dry, clutched tightly in damp hands. Yes, meeting a lender for the first time can be a trying experience if you don't get yourself into the right mind-set before the appointment.

The important thing to remember is that you are not asking for a handout; you are applying for a loan. That's a business plan in your hand, not a tin cup. Think and act accordingly. Don't unintentionally denigrate your business by using qualifiers to describe it. Statements like, "It's only a small home business," or, "I'm pretty sure I can make a go of it," are not the phrases that win a lender's favor. It is surprising how often would-be business people use just this kind of language when they speak to a banker. Chances are that they will stay in the "would-be" category forever. Don't be one of them.

Approach your target banker with precision and poise. If you have done your research and thought through your plan, you are ready. Don't doubt yourself or your right to apply for funding. Without the small, enterprising business person, there would be a lot fewer bankers sitting behind those desks. It's a good idea to remember that.

Professional lenders know that they need you just as much as you need them. You are two business people working toward the same goal — the development of a successful enterprise. While you can't afford to be arrogant in your dealings with your banker, you can approach him or her as an equal in the world of commerce. If you are prepared, courteous, and act in a straightforward manner, there is no doubt that the impression you leave with the banker will be a positive one.

The human species is composed of two distinct races: the men who borrow, and the men who lend.

Charles Lamb

h. What to do if the banker says no

Most successful business people have been turned down by a lender at some time in their careers. If your first attempt to raise funds is unsuccessful, don't view it as the end of the line. Turn it into a positive learning experience.

Ask the banker why the loan wasn't approved. The explanation he or she gives you may well be just the information you need to ensure that you are successful the second, or even third time out. Query him or her on why your application was rejected. Ask if your business plan was lacking some necessary information. Was the problem in your forecast? Was it your market research? Don't let the loan rejection blind you to the opportunity to learn and perhaps improve your presentation.

You will find that once a banker has refused a loan, and that refusal has been regretfully (but graciously) accepted, the pressure is off. Few people don't like to give advice when asked for it; a lender is no exception. So don't rush from the bank like a beaten puppy. Stay for a time; a friendly talk could prove worthwhile.

A *thoughtful pause*

You move now from the planning phase of your venture to the active phase of running a business operation. You begin to organize your space needs, produce your product or service, develop your selling skills, work with customers, and start record keeping. In the months to come, you will become completely involved in the task of managing and growing your home-based business. How you do it will be up to you, for the enterprise you create is yours, and it will bear your personal stamp.

The planning phase of any business has locked-in requirements: the need to assess your skills, to set goals, to research your market, and to forecast your cash. As a homepreneur, you have the added task of gaining (and keeping!) family support while organizing the home environment so that it can include your enterprise with minimal disruption.

Running your business demands the same skills used in the planning process — and more. To grow and prosper, it needs your dedication, creativity, and persistence in full measure. It will demand your best.

Before you start on the next phase, stop for a minute. Visualize four things lying on the floor: a wooden seat and three wooden legs — the makings of a stool. If you want to sit safely and comfortably on the stool, the three legs must be securely attached to the seat so that it can properly support your weight.

Your business is just such a stool. The three legs are marketing, administration, and finance. Every business, no matter how small, is comprised of these three elements. With even one missing, the stool will not support itself.

- Marketing: It's obvious — without sales there is no business.
- Administration: To succeed, you must plan and control your enterprise. Records must be kept and systems monitored.

- Finance: Understanding and seeing to the cash needs of your business is a continuing task.

As you go about building your home-based business, keep the three legs of the stool fixed in your mind. Every decision you make will in some way involve each of them. Give each leg the time and consideration it deserves to ensure the stool remains strong.

Now let's get on with it.

8

Organizing your working space

Every cubic inch of space is a miracle.

Walt Whitman

In the famous television series *Star Trek,* space is described as the final frontier. For the home-based business person, it is the first frontier. You can work on the kitchen or dining room table for only so long before this becomes painfully obvious.

The space needs of every business are unique. Big corporations spend thousands, sometimes millions, of dollars to plan and furnish their office and production facilities. Experts are hired, coordinators assigned, and tasks delegated, all to ensure that the working space is adequate and functional. Large, sophisticated businesses are aware of the correlation of space planning to productivity.

You, on the other hand, will be forced to compromise, adjust, and to a great extent force your business to conform to an existing structure, your home. It may be ideal; usually it is not. What is important is that the area you choose provide enough space and privacy to conduct your business.

Home-based businesses can occupy an attic, spare bedroom, a little-used dining room, a basement, or a converted garage. I recently read of a home-based enterprise set up in the owners' indoor pool area. They drained the pool, built a floor over it, and there it was — space enough for their home-based real estate company. Not too many of us have indoor pool areas to convert, but with a little imagination and a lot of ingenuity, we can usually find space enough to meet our needs.

a. What will you need?

The nature of the business dictates what space you need and how it should be outfitted. Ask yourself the following questions:

(a) Will I be working alone, or will I have employees? You may not have employees at the start, but hiring them later may be a possibility. If the spare room you've claimed for your office cannot easily accommodate another person, look around for extra space you can use if you have to.

(b) Do I need my space to act as a showroom for my product? If you're planning to entertain or sell to customers from your home, the space should have a professional image. Check the route to your office/showroom from your front door. If your customer has to pass through the laundry room or children's playroom, you will have to consider this in your plan.

(c) Do I have tools or utensils that must be kept safely out of the reach of children? You may require special storage racks or enclosed cupboards to ensure your family's safety. This is important not only for your own children but for their inquisitive friends.

(d) What are my electrical requirements? Chances are that you will require more electrical outlets than the average home provides. The wealth of technology available to the homepreneur includes things such as computers, copiers, fax machines, etc. They all need to be plugged in somewhere. You may want to discuss your power needs with an electrician before you start. Depending on what your equipment demands, you might need to add extra circuits to take the additional load.

If you are planning to use a computer, you may want to consider a dedicated circuit, a

PROPERLY DESIGNED FURNITURE AND EQUIPMENT CONTRIBUTE TO YOUR EFFICIENCY AND EFFECTIVENESS.

current line reserved specifically for the computer with no household appliance use. This eliminates unwanted power drains and surges from start-and-stop appliances such as coffee pots, washing machines, or refrigerators. Such changes in the level of power going to your computer can cause damage to both the system itself and the stored information. Small power surges may not have the instant effect of a bolt of lightning, but damage does accumulate over time.

You should also use a surge protector to protect such sensitive equipment from power surges that come from *outside* your home. Electricity does not flow to our homes in an unbroken stream. Storms, utility company repair operations, or "brown outs" all cause changes in power transmission. Without protection from such changes in voltage, electronic equipment can be severely damaged. Surge protectors, which look much like standard extension cords, are available in hardware stores and computer supply shops for under $20. They should also be used for any communications equipment such as modems or fax machines.

(e) What are my lighting requirements? Your area of activity is a place of serious work. It should have proper lighting. You will probably need more light than the average spare room or attic will provide. Poor light leads to headaches, eyestrain, and low productivity, so make sure your lighting is adequate.

(f) Do I have any special needs — for extra plumbing, inventory storage, shelving? Make a list of any special needs your business has and keep it handy as you do your space planning. If your business involves food preparation, for example, you might need refrigeration or counter space.

(g) Are there extra ventilation or air conditioning requirements? That spare bedroom you've decided to use for your office might turn into an oven during the summer and have little or no air movement. If you use equipment that generates heat, it will add to the burden. You can't work in hot, dead air — not for long, anyway. If you can't afford air conditioning, you might try a fan.

(h) Is the area free of noise disturbance? You will want some protection from noise if you live in an active household. While soft background music can be a welcome sound, you may not feel the same if your 14-year-old decides on some high volume heavy metal after school.

Conversely, if in the process of doing your work, you make noise that would irritate other members of the family, you might want to install some soundproofing. Don't try for total silence, as you will probably find a complete lack of sound as disconcerting as too much of it. A happy medium is all that is required.

b. Space planning

Once you have selected the area of your home to use for your business, do some planning. You want the space to be as functional and attractive as possible. With a little thought before you set up your space, you increase your chance of achieving the results you want. By planning, not only will your task be easier, but you will also avoid costly mistakes.

1. Clean house

The first thing to do is find sufficient storage for the items displaced to make room for your new office. This can be a challenge! Do not try to *save* everything taken out of the room. You will simply cram the rest of the house with items that serve no real purpose and detract from your home decor. The home-based business person can't afford to be a pack rat, so if you can, get rid of everything you do not absolutely need. Try to create as much empty space as possible. Consider a garage sale to earn some extra dollars for your new business furniture.

2. Measure the space

When the room is empty, take accurate measurements and produce a plan of the space as it is at present. You can purchase graph paper for this purpose at any stationery store. Draw the space to scale (say, ½ inch to a foot or 1 cm to 25 cm). Mark existing electrical outlets, lighting placement, heating units, and any other unique characteristics of the room such as stair wells or closets. After you have done this, you can begin to change the old space into the new space your business needs.

3. List your office needs

Make a list of the furniture, equipment, and supplies you need to start your business. Beside each major item make a note of its dimensions. Indicate whether it requires electricity or has special power requirements. These are important planning steps; don't bypass them. You will be frustrated and annoyed if you find you have not allowed space enough for furniture or misjudged your electrical requirements. If you are unsure about measurements, visit a few showrooms and take a tape measure. If you've ordered equipment, ask the supplier for accurate dimensions.

Easily forgotten and often underestimated is the space required for filing cabinets or storage. Use Worksheet #12 and make your list as complete as possible. It will form the basis for your office space plan.

4. *Choose the right furniture*

You are on a budget, and there is no need to spend one cent more than necessary to produce an attractive, serviceable work area. But the furniture you choose should be selected to serve you well. Properly designed furniture and equipment contribute to your efficiency and effectiveness in running your business.

If you throw a home workplace together with leftover odds and sods, it may do for a short time, but when the rickety chair causes lower back pain and the drawers of your desk constantly stick or fall apart, you will not be comfortable, and you will not be productive. Don't create a place of work that you will dread going into three months from start up. It will encourage you to procrastinate and your business will suffer. When shopping for your office, check out the local suppliers of used office furniture. In most medium to large cities, they abound. Some very good prices can be had on furniture, filing cabinets, and storage units that may be used but are not necessarily old. Bear in mind that standard desk and chair heights have been carefully researched to ensure a high degree of comfort. Remember, you want to create a professional and productive business setting, not a torture chamber.

5. *Draw a plan*

Planning first on paper gives you the opportunity to visualize your new office as it should be. All too often, homepreneurs rush out, buy a desk, chair, or filing cabinet, and bring it home. Only then do they discover that the item is too large and cumbersome for the space available. They either live with it, using space they desperately need later, or have to try to return the item to the supplier. If the goods were purchased as used, this can often be difficult — sometimes impossible.

Planning your business space on paper helps you avoid such costly mistakes. It's a lot easier to move furniture with pencil and eraser than with muscle.

It's a good thing that when God created the rainbow He didn't consult a decorator or He would still be picking colors.

Sam Levenson

Worksheet #12
List of furniture and equipment

ITEM	MEASUREMENT	POWER?
_____	_____ X _____	_____
_____	_____ X _____	_____
_____	_____ X _____	_____
_____	_____ X _____	_____
_____	_____ X _____	_____
_____	_____ X _____	_____
_____	_____ X _____	_____
_____	_____ X _____	_____
_____	_____ X _____	_____
_____	_____ X _____	_____
_____	_____ X _____	_____
_____	_____ X _____	_____
_____	_____ X _____	_____
_____	_____ X _____	_____
_____	_____ X _____	_____
_____	_____ X _____	_____
_____	_____ X _____	_____
_____	_____ X _____	_____

Do I have enough storage?_____

Do I have enough filing capacity?_____

What is the total number of electrical outlets needed?_____

Do I have enough working surface?_____

When you make your plan, draw the major items first — things such as desks, electrical equipment, and storage cupboards. Try them in different positions in the plan until you find the arrangement that gives the best use of the available space.

6. *Storage — and more storage*

Homepreneurs agree. There is never enough. "Plan for your storage needs, then double it," was the advice of one successful home business person.

Businesses create bulk. It comes in the form of stationery, office supplies, inventory, display materials, business records, and other paraphernalia associated with the enterprise. Left unchecked, it overwhelms both you and your working area, and keeping it under control is a constant challenge.

Don't underestimate your storage needs. Check your home for hidden space that can be used for excess storage. Consider a little-used closet where clothes racks could be replaced with inexpensive shelving. What about taking over part of the garage if lack of heat will not damage the stored goods. The basement is also a possibility.

Separate items that need storage into two groups: those that need to be close by and those that don't. Try not to clutter up your home office with materials or goods that don't need to be there. This is particularly important if you entertain customers at your home business. Don't make them think they are doing business in a disorganized warehouse. The impression you create can make or break their confidence in you as a business person.

Many home-based business people use storage outside the home, particularly when the business carries a lot of inventory or the materials used are bulky. The added cost of using a mini-storage facility near your home may be the answer if your home space is limited.

7. *Lighting up*

While your working area does not need to have the light of a summer day at high noon, lighting should be of good quality and properly located. Poor quality in lighting causes fatigue, eye strain, and, over time, eye damage. You will spend a lot of time working under the lights in your new office or shop so it's a good idea to plan for your personal comfort and eye safety.

Studies prove that bad lighting has an adverse affect on both mood and behavior, while good lighting improves productivity and contributes to a sense of well-being. Shadowy, uneven lighting is especially tiring. Pay particular attention to areas of your work space where close, concentrated work will be done, and be sure they are adequately lit. By adding some track lighting or inexpensive clamp-on lamps, you will feel better about your work and be more efficient. For this type of lighting a dimmer switch that allows you some control is helpful.

Offices use fluorescent lighting for its ability to light without shadows, an important consideration for eye comfort. The quality of fluorescent light has improved in past years. The use of pink tone eliminates the look of a hospital ward at midnight. Fluorescent lighting is also more energy efficient than the incandescent light normally used in homes, and it will last up to 20 times longer. Consider fluorescent light if your work demands that you move constantly between one area of the room and another.

8. *A word about decor*

This is a business book, not a decorating book, and I won't tell you how to decorate your office; it is a matter of personal taste. If you will never be entertaining a customer, your decorating decisions can be as outlandish and off-the-wall as you want. Do what will work for you.

However, it's a different story if you plan to bring clients or customers to your home office. You are striving to build a business, to be taken seriously, and to encourage a strong relationship with your customers or clients. The image you project through your home office makes an important contribution to those objectives. Create a background for doing business. Let your work environment show that you are serious and organized about the tasks at hand. This does not mean that you sacrifice your own taste. It merely suggests that you take your customer's impressions into consideration.

Create a workplace of both style and substance, a workplace that you look forward to being in and hate to leave. If you can do that, both you and your business will benefit.

c. *Why your working environment matters*

One of the greatest challenges for a home-based business person is to sustain a dedicated sense of purpose. Often he or she is plagued with self-doubt and has only a fragile, easily eroded perception of himself or herself as a "real" business person. A well-planned home office goes a long way toward fostering a more positive sense of worth.

Be good to yourself. Create a workplace of both style and substance, a workplace that you look forward to being in and hate to leave. If you can do that, both you and your business will benefit.

9

Marketing

The purpose of a business is to get and keep a customer.

Theodore Levitt

This is the most important chapter in the book. There, I've said it. No matter how you produce, control, manage, or administrate your product or service, it will sit on the shelves if you can't persuade someone to buy it. Does this statement negate everything written in the other sections of this book? No. All the other activities are designed — and necessary — to ensure the selling process is profitable. You *sell* your product or service to have a business; you *control* the process to have profits.

In the early days of a business, success — and survival — depend completely on selling.

It is difficult to emphasize the marketing and selling process without diminishing the importance of the administration and financial processes, but emphasis it must have if you are to succeed. Experts say that in the early days of a business, success — and survival — depend completely on selling. Every aspect of your business is important, but the selling function is critical. Whether your business lives or dies depends on it.

a. Marketing options

There are many ways that business people try to reach and sell to their customers: telephone, mail order, advertising, and personal sales to name a few. As your home business changes and grows, you may experiment with each of them before you find what will work best for you. In the early days of most businesses, the most direct route to a sale is through personal contact, meeting and talking to as many people as you can and persuading them to buy your service or product.

You are not an organization with layers of management or support staff to help you build your enterprise. The contract for the goods or services you provide to your customer is a personal one. Therefore, your business will depend on the rapport you develop with that customer, and the creation of a harmonious relationship that will benefit each of you.

The home-based business person more than any other has the chance to develop a strong personal bond with customers or clients. You do, after all, invite them to your home — what can be more personal than that?

The opportunity to build such a relationship in this impersonal world is what I call a grand advantage. It is an advantage that the smart homepreneur capitalizes on. As we move through this chapter, we will cover some methods of selling your product, but let's begin with that grand advantage: personal sales. Start by meeting as many people as you can.

b. Building your network

Selling involves making direct calls on potential customers, and it is made easier and more enjoyable by a determined effort to network. Networking paves the way to sales by helping you target your efforts. It can open doors that might otherwise be closed to you. It also helps you overcome the fear of rejection that often sabotages the efforts of untrained salespeople. A commitment to personal sales as the means to launch your new business should include a commitment to networking.

1. What is a network?

A network is a group of business contacts — people you meet and associate with for mutual support, the exchange of business information, and developing and creating new business. The underlying objective of networking is to increase your chances of making sales by expanding your list of business contacts.

Networking is a natural function of the human race. It starts the day we are born. Our first network is small: mother, father, brothers, sisters, etc. The network enlarges when we go to school, college, or university and our circle of friends and companions increases. It expands again when we enter the workplace, meeting and interacting with new people. Each new undertaking opens the door to another network and each network plays a crucial role in the success and development of a business.

Planning to be a business person without a network is like climbing a high mountain without a team. Not only is the climb more difficult, perhaps even impossible, it's lonely when you reach the peak.

Networks can be formal associations or informal groups. Their goals can be stringently defined as in some international trade networks or much less formal as in a group of salespeople who get together over an early breakfast to exchange leads. Networking organizations abound in North America and cover almost every aspect of business. There are specific networks for women in business, sales personnel, and presidents of large corporations. There are also networks for home-based business people. The common goal of the professional network is to ensure that each participant benefits from the relationship according to what he or she contributes.

Networking plays an important role in the growth of a business. It provides sources of new business, offers opportunities to share business problems and concerns with others, and helps the business person realize that he or she is not alone. Networking also allows you to learn from people who have been down the same path, and provides a sounding board for ideas and plans. Networking benefits you and your business by keeping you current, constantly exposing you to new ideas and making you aware of developments in your industry of choice. It has a side effect, too. When you need information, nothing is more satisfying than being able to pick up the phone, call a business associate from your network, and get the answers you seek.

It is a truism, as a friend and successful business person once told me, that "people do business with people," not corporations, not companies, but people. If you accept this, and I hope you do, plan to meet and talk with as many people as you can. Broaden your network, join, and participate. Not only is it good for you, it's good for business.

2. Choosing your network

I won't belong to any organization that would have me as a member.

Groucho Marx

While every organization and network provides the opportunity to meet people and exchange those all-important business cards, some are better than others. Depending on your type of business, you may think it best to belong only to a local group or perhaps a highly select one. There's no law that says you can't check out the group before you join.

Most networks have a spokesperson who can answer questions about the group's goals and objectives. Call first, describe your business, and tell them what you're looking for from membership in a network organization. Often, you will be invited to attend an introductory meeting so you can see first hand how the group operates. This is always worthwhile, particularly if you're not sure which group is right for you. Even if you decide not to join, you'll meet people and have an interesting hour or two. If you have the time, there's nothing to stop you from joining more than one network. The more networking you do the greater the chance to increase sales.

Don't waste your networking efforts by not keeping notes and records unless you have the memory of an elephant. The easiest way to do it is to keep a business card file, which you can buy at any stationery shop. Many people develop the habit, and it's a good one, of making short notes about other business people they meet. They record the date, where the meeting took place, and any additional information that will help them remember the person or business. Sometimes the note is just a line or two on the back of the business card before they file it. It's a good spur for the memory a few months and a few hundred business cards later.

3. *Developing your own network*

Every person you meet and communicate with expands your network. Networking needn't always be formal. You can learn and profit, both in a personal and business sense, from suppliers, competitors, other business owners, and your own customers if you take the time to lift the relationship to a new level. Never assume that a person who is working in another industry can't help your business. If that person can't help directly, there's always a chance that he or she knows someone who can.

The reason for networking is the *exchange* of information. If you meet a person who may be a potential networking partner, tell him or her what business you are in, but don't sell — tell. Two-way communication is what you are after. Try not to endanger a possibly beneficial long-term relationship by being pushy. A major show of ego about what *you* are doing, what *you* think, and what *your* plans are will turn off another business person — quickly and permanently. Besides, he or she may have something to say that will be of value to you and your business. If your mouth is open and your ears closed, you'll miss it.

Ask questions about the other person's business, show a genuine interest, and if you think of something helpful, a sales lead or some new information, pass it along. That's what networking is all about.

Networking for the home-based business person has value beyond potential sales. It keeps you informed, contributes to your profits, and perhaps, most important of all, it keeps you motivated and boosts creativity. With a strong circle of business associates, it is easier to beat those feelings of isolation that often trouble the person working at home. Just pick up the phone and make a lunch date.

Information on home-based business networks is available through various newsletters. You do not have to be a member of a network organization to subscribe to the newsletters, and subscription rates are nominal — usually between $18 and $45 annually. Write to one or both of the following organizations. Both publish excellent newsletters for the home-based worker.

Barbara Brabec's Self-Employment Survival Newsletter
Barbara Brabec's Productions
P.O. Box 2137
Naperville, IL 60467

Barbara Mowat, Publisher
Home Business Report
2949 Ash Street
Abbotsford, BC V2S 4G5
E-mail: hbr@cyberstore.ca
Internet: http://www.bcyellowpages.com/news/
           home_office/index.html

These organizations provide topical, pertinent information for the home-based worker and are especially useful in keeping you informed of upcoming home-based business shows and seminars. Don't miss these chances to learn, meet, and mingle.

Also consider joining the American Home-Business Association (HBA). The association publishers a magazine, *Home Business News*, quarterly and the *HBA Hotline Newsletter* eight times a year. The publications are upbeat and useful, filled with articles and tips to help you run your business better. Membership also entitles you to discounts on office products, travel, health insurance, and more. For more information, you can reach the association by phone (1-800-664-2422), fax (801-273-5422), or e-mail (infor@homebusiness.com). If you have access to the Net, you can view their Web site at *http://www.homebusiness.com*.

c. *Direct selling*

Direct selling ranks right up there with public speaking when it comes to generating fear and trepidation among many would-be home-preneurs. Some experts say that fear of selling often stops otherwise talented people from ever starting a business of their own. Instead, they dream about finding or creating a product that will "sell itself." A pleasant fantasy, but an unlikely reality. If the idea of selling makes you nervous, take heart. While selling ability may come easier to some people than others, it is not a divine gift, and *it can be learned*. Begin with desire and motivation, add some organization and dedication and a liberal dose of common sense, and you have it.

1. *Finding the customers*

It is probably no accident that the word used in business to define the search for customers is prospecting. The word conjures up images of gold and rightly so. A satisfied customer is pure gold to any business. Some people might say that the process of finding prospects is equally as difficult as mining that elusive ore. It need not be, if you approach it systematically.

Think about who your potential customers are. Call to mind every person, group, or commercial business that might use your product or service. Try to visualize the customers specifically. Ask yourself questions about them. How old are they? What business are they in? Ask questions that personalize them in your mind. Thinking about who your customers are will lead you to understand their buying motives. Having a sense of why they buy will help you later in developing advertising and more directly targeting your market. Try to give your customers shapes and faces you recognize. Think about every possible use for your product or service and *see* people buying and using it. Fill in Worksheet #13 to help you do this.

Think about where you will find them. If your potential customers are pet store owners, it may be as uncomplicated as looking in your local Yellow Pages. If they are harder to pinpoint, check out organizations and trade associations or any other groups that a potential customer might be involved in.

Thinking creatively about *who* your customers are will help to tell you *where* they are. Don't forget that a good prospect is *any* person, business, or group that might buy what you are selling. Try to expand your thinking to include prospects you might otherwise have overlooked. On Worksheet #14, answer the question, "Where will I find my customers?"

You've done some real work here, so don't forget to write it down. At this point, you should have no difficulty making a preliminary list of potential customers for your new business. It may not contain a million names, but it is a place to start.

2. *Keeping prospect records*

Open a file, either manually or on your trusty computer, and call it PROSPECTS. Design a format that suits you, but be sure it contains all pertinent information. Many salespeople prefer to keep their prospect and sales call data on small file cards. They carry the active cards with them when they make their calls. After each appointment, they make notes on them: date of call, person contacted, etc. When they return to the office, they refile them. Other professionals use a standard three-ring binder. They keep current prospects with them and file the rest.

Whatever method you choose, be sure to leave space on the sheet for your personal comments and date every entry. Leave some space to write notes that will help you build a relationship with that customer. For example, you might write, "She just got a promotion." "She likes to sail." "He likes to ski." This kind of data personalizes the relationship and encourages rapport. As a sales-call opener, it beats talking about the weather. Also make notes about what you learned about the company. Examples: "The company is expanding. It is opening a new branch [or closing one.]" "There's a new general manager." Write down anything that increases your knowledge of the prospect. Sample #4 shows one person's method of keeping such records.

d. Develop a sales attitude

If you don't consider yourself a salesperson, you may be dreading that first call on a potential customer. Ask yourself what causes the dread. What is the reason for your attitude?

Perhaps you harbor negative images of salespeople. You may think they are somewhat unsavory characters determined to make a sale at any cost and willing to bend the truth to do it. You don't want either you or your business tarnished by such an image. Because you have this attitude, you assume the customer has it, too.

Some salespeople do act unprofessionally and some have questionable ethics, but if you look hard at the truly successful ones, you'll see that these qualities are noticeably absent. Honest, professional

Worksheet #13
Who is my customer?

Describe who you think your customer is and why he or she might buy your product. On the right, make notes of any other significant facts about your customers.

NOTES:

Age group: _____   _____

Sex: _____   _____

Marital status: _____   _____

Income: _____   _____

Type of employment: _____

    Professional_____   _____

    Academic _____   _____

    Office _____   _____

    Other _____   _____

Where do they live?   _____

_____   _____

What do they buy now? (luxury,   _____

budget, image, convenience, service)   _____

_____   _____

What do they join?   _____

(clubs, organizations, networks)   _____

_____   _____

Why will they buy from me?   _____

_____   _____

Geographic location:

Local_____

National_____

Other_____

If my customers are commercial (i.e., other businesses) are they:

Downtown_____

Nearby_____

Suburbs_____

Where would I be most likely to meet them?

_____

_____

If I am selling directly to the consumer, how do they shop?

Convenience	_____	Cash or credit card	_____
Mail order	_____	Discount	_____
Impulse	_____	Telephone	_____

Where would I be most likely to meet them?

_____

_____

NOTES:

_____

_____

_____

_____

_____

_____

Sample #4
Prospect sheet

Date:_____

Company name:_____Telephone number:_____

Address:_____

_____

Contact name:_____

Title:_____

Type of business:_____

Comments:_____

_____

_____

_____

_____

_____

_____

_____

_____

_____

_____

_____

_____

_____

salespeople have a strong sense of ethics and a genuine desire to provide quality goods and services. Their kind of selling is a respectable *and respected* activity.

So get rid of your negative feelings. Decide to do sales your way — the right way.

Ask yourself the following questions:

(a) Am I proud of the product or service I offer the customer?

(b) Will I do the best job possible?

(c) Will I always deal honestly with my customer?

(d) Am I entitled to a fair profit for my efforts?

(e) Does my product or service give good value to the customer?

(f) Am I selling quality?

(g) Will I stand behind what I sell?

(h) Do I believe the customer has a right to good service?

The ability to sell begins with a strong belief in what you are selling. If you answered yes to the above questions, there is no reason for you not to be positive and confident as you begin the selling and marketing process for your home-based business. When you believe in what you are doing and respect the customer's right to a fair exchange, their money for your goods, the selling process is made honorable and greatly simplified.

e. The introductory call

Your first call on a prospective client is the easiest one you'll ever make. Why? Because you're not going to *sell* anything — not directly anyway. You're going to give him or her information about you and your business, and you're going to ask for some information in return. You're simply going to introduce yourself. What could be easier than that? (If you do find yourself with an order or two, try not to act too astonished.)

Your introductory calls provide the opportunity to learn and use basic selling techniques. As your business grows and your sales effort becomes more sophisticated, you will be surprised to find out that you are already expert in 90% of the skills required for successful sales just from making your introductory calls. You may even have trouble remembering why you were nervous in the first place.

For effective calls follow this simple plan:

(a) Make a list of the potential customers you want to see and use it to prioritize your calls. Make it easier by grouping the calls by address. Try not to be running all over town during rush hour. Time is a resource and it's a shame to waste it sitting in traffic if you can plan to avoid it.

(b) Once you have settled on the prospects to call on, put yourself on a schedule. Consider the time you have available, and then decide how many calls you can make in a day, a week, or a month. Plan to complete all your introductory calls in a set amount of time — and stick to your plan. No procrastination allowed. It helps to set aside specific days for your calls. This makes it easier to manage your time.

(c) Focus your call. Try to make good use of your time by ensuring that you speak to the right person. If you have prospected thoroughly, you will avoid the possibility of talking to a clerk at the front desk when you should be seeing the owner or manager. If you are more comfortable with scheduled appointments, make them.

(d) Be brief. The introductory call should be brief and to the point. The aim is to establish contact, not to apply sales pressure. This rule is flexible. If a customer wants specific information and appears interested in what you have to say, seize the moment. Take the time necessary to answer his or her queries. (To prepare for this magic moment, read section **f.** below.)

(e) Express interest in what the prospect does. The introductory call is an opportunity not only to tell about your business, but to learn about the customer's. Show interest and enthusiasm about what he or she is doing, and you will gain valuable insight into what the customer might require from you. Listen — and hear. Information is a precious resource.

(f) Dress appropriately. When you make a call, you are representing your business. How you look and the image you create will be important and create a lasting impression. You don't need a thousand-dollar suit; in fact, unless you are selling into the luxury market, dressing too expensively might work against you. But you do need to look professional.

(g) Always leave something behind. Chances are that your potential customers are busy people. If you rely solely on their memory, you may be disappointed. Try to leave something behind that will help them remember you were there. A business card? Of course. But it's a good idea to leave more: a short brochure telling what your home-based business does or even a crisp, typewritten page of information. If you have made a good impression and if your product or service holds some interest for the customer, it's a pretty good bet that the information will get filed for future reference.

(h) Thank your prospects for their time. Common courtesy is a winning factor in all human relations. Business is no exception. People's time is valuable. If they give some to you by listening to your company story, be sure you thank them for it.

(i) Smile. The smile is often forgotten in the bustle of commerce, despite its universal power to encourage friendship and trust. Consider this a gentle reminder.

(j) Follow up the call. A short note, again thanking the person for seeing you, is a positive way of reminding him or her you were there. The cost of postage is paltry compared to the benefits of expressing your thanks in writing and setting your product or service firmly in the customer's mind. For an example of such a letter see Sample #5.

(k) Keep a record. When you are just starting out, you think you will remember everything. You often do, for the first month or two, but it's a good idea not to trust your memory too completely. Pick up a business card from the person you see, and if there are company brochures available ask for one. Keep notes and records on all your customer contacts from the very beginning and always date them.

f. Selling tips

They gave each other a smile with a future in it.
Ring Lardner

The first essential key to selling is to develop a sensitivity to your potential customer, and that is not always a simple task.

Each of us is a unique creature. However, we do share some likes and dislikes. We respond to people who are courteous, for example, and we are repelled by actions that are overbearing or ungracious. We respect honesty and upstanding behavior and deplore deceit. And we all like to be treated with respect. These likes and dislikes underlie all human relationships and understanding them is crucial in the selling process. Sensitivity to them is part of the art of persuasion.

January 15, 200-

Mr. Smith
Director of Marketing
ABC Company Inc.
12345 Prospect Row
Vancouver, BC Z1P 0G0

Dear Mr. Smith:

Thank you for taking the time to meet with me last Thursday. I know your days are busy, and that makes me doubly appreciate the interest you expressed in my company.

If Marin Consulting can ever be of service to you, please let me know. The opportunity to work with you would be a pleasure.

Again, my thanks.

Sincerely,

Kit Jones
President

With that in mind, here are some basic selling tips:

(a) Be prepared, which means knowing your product and being able to answer any questions that pertain to it. Being prepared means not having to rifle through your briefcase for sales literature and then, heaven forbid, coming up empty. Being prepared means producing a business card when asked and not having to write your business name and telephone number on a scrap of paper. Being prepared means never having to say you're sorry.

(b) Don't talk too much. Know when to speak and when not to. Don't be afraid of silence. It could mean the person across the desk is deciding to buy your product. You cannot force a sale by using a million words, but you can lose one.

(c) Show genuine interest. I've already said this, but it bears repeating. It is basic to human nature that we are drawn to people who show interest in us. Part of any sales call is social in nature. Use this time to establish a rapport with your potential customer.

When you call on someone, see him or her first as *a person*, and only then as a customer. While you are not in a position to interrogate the person, you can ask friendly questions if your interest is sincere. What do you do? How long have you been with the company? Where are you from? These questions are all appropriate if they are asked in a friendly manner. Showing interest in the potential customer is the polite way to conduct business.

Speaking of politeness — please don't use a customer's first name on an initial call unless specifically asked to do so. If you are a smoker, don't ask to smoke, and strive diligently to avoid the bright, breezy, and *very trite* "and how are you today?" opener.

(d) Avoid questions that can be answered yes or no. One of the objectives of a good sales call is to establish a dialogue. To do this it helps to stick with open-ended questions that require a response, not a decision. This is a helpful guide when making appointments as well. Look at these examples.

Question: Could I make an appointment to see you on July 22 at 10:00 a.m.?

Answer: No.

Wouldn't it be better this way?

Question: I would like to make an appointment to see you. When would be the best time?

Answer: "Hm-m, let me see. Sometime next week, maybe.

Question: Is there a particular day that would be good for you?

I think you get the idea. By asking a question that avoids a yes or no answer, you have a better chance of accomplishing your objective.

(e) Be honest. It is counter-productive to lie to make a sale. It doesn't do any good to be evasive either. Always remember that you are trying to build a long-term relationship. You might get one big order with one small lie, but if that lie is discovered you will have destroyed the long-term success of your business. And believe me, lies do get found out eventually.

(f) Don't overstay your welcome. Knowing when to leave shows courtesy and respect. If you have booked a 15-minute appointment, stick to your time. Break this rule only if asked to. Try not to wait until the potential customer is nervously shuffling desk papers and glancing at a clock.

(g) Assume the customer will buy and ask for the order. Amazingly enough, one of biggest mistakes made by new salespeople is failure to ask for the order. Asking for the order is like hitting the wall for most first-time salespeople — perhaps because it is the one question that by its nature demands a yes or no answer. Don't let it stop you.

Asking for the order is a perfectly logical and acceptable thing to do. It is expected. You are not there under false pretenses; the customer knows you are there to make a sale. Deciding on the right moment to ask the question is the most difficult thing. If the meeting has gone well, the customer has expressed solid interest, and you have dealt with any negative factors, the time is probably opportune. Consider using a closing comment like this:

"I hope I've answered all your questions, Mr. Smith, and I really appreciate the interest you've shown in the product. Can I write up an order? Delivery would be in about a week."

If your business is a service, try this:

"I hope I've answered all your questions, Mr. Smith, and I really appreciate all the interest you have shown. You mentioned that you'll be needing your carpets cleaned in about another two months. Can we set up a schedule for that now? I'd like to make the time as convenient for you as possible."

(h) Leave on a high note. This is easy if you made the sale. The handshake is firm, the smiles are warm, and the order is signed. It is more a test of your mettle if you met with refusal. If the call is unsuccessful, don't let it show. Keep the handshake firm and the smile warm, and be sure to leave the door open. If you were professional, well-intentioned, and honest, that customer will see you again. In sales, there is always another day.

g. *Why won't you sell?*

The new business person has other reasons for hesitating to call on customers: doubts about selling ability, fear of rejection, or just plain shyness. Such personal feelings are obstacles to the success of your enterprise, but they can be overcome.

Giving in to a lack of confidence, fear of rejection, or timidity means that you *will not* sell, and if you will not sell, you won't be in business very long. While selling comes more easily to some than to others, competent selling techniques can be learned and your personal barriers can be overcome.

1. *Doubting your sales ability*

If you doubt your ability to sell, chances are that you say to yourself, "I'm just not a sales type." You may believe that in order to sell you have to turn yourself inside out and act in a way that goes against your basic nature. Not so. You do not have to become someone else to communicate with a prospective client. It's probably the worst thing that you could do!

Be yourself when you talk to a customer. You have a better chance of being remembered. You know how to be courteous, you know what your product is, your intention is honorable (to provide quality and service), and you know how to smile. That's all you need. If you want more examples to build your confidence just look around at the people you see making their living by selling. They're a mixed group, aren't they? There's a strong message there — you can stay you and still be successful in sales.

2. *Fear of rejection*

People who are inexperienced in sales often take all rejection personally. If a customer says, "I don't want it," the salesperson translates it to mean, "*I'm* not wanted," or, "This person doesn't like *me*." The only way to beat fear of rejection is to accept right off that the customer has the right not to buy and that many times he or she *will* say those two terrible words: "no thanks."

There are probably a thousand reasons why he or she won't buy, and probably none of them relates to you personally. Maybe he was bitten by a dog that morning; maybe she bought the same thing last week; maybe they both simply don't want what you are selling. If you accept rejection as a natural part of the selling process, it loses its ability to hold you back. Rejection is a fact. You will experience it. Not everyone will buy your product or service. On occasion they may even be less than courteous. Rejection is not life threatening, so keep it in perspective and carry on.

3. *Shyness*

You're just plain shy? Most people are to some degree. But shyness can be beaten. The shy person overcomes the fear of selling by continually building on a strong desire to achieve an objective. If the desire is strong enough, willpower *will* see you through.

Every time you approach a prospective customer, have your goal in mind. Think about your business, not yourself, and the task will be easier. In many ways, the shy person often has an advantage over more extroverted colleagues, an advantage that is often overlooked. If you are shy by nature, chances are that you have developed a natural talent for listening, and that skill is a salesperson's most powerful tool. Use it.

Overcoming your shyness takes a bit of backbone, but you can do it if you really want to. Anais Nin once said, "Life shrinks or expands in proportion to one's courage." So will your business.

h. *Help yourself sell*

You can never know enough about sales and marketing. It is the most dynamic process within your enterprise. After you have made a few introductory calls, you will realize that the same rules apply to all the calls you make. Most of these rules can be learned. Please plan on taking some sales training. While you can and should learn all you can from the many books available, do check courses and

Anais Nin once said, "Life shrinks or expands in proportion to one's courage." So will your business.

seminars. Your local chamber of commerce, board of trade, or local college are all good sources for information on sales training schedules and events.

Watch the business section of your local paper for special sales seminars that may be coming to your community. Many of these seminars train and motivate. As your awareness and skill grow, so will your confidence. Your apprehension about selling will be more easily overcome if you meet and mingle with other people striving for the same objective.

A few short pages cannot cover all the options. Just let me prod you to learn as much as you can about the art of persuasion, and then get out there and sell. Meet and talk to as many potential customers as you can. Learn to put your message across in a clear and winning style. Believe that what you do has merit and become adept at the art of persuading others to agree with you. Don't say, "I can't" or "I won't." Such words imply a luxury of choice that you, as a start-up homepreneur, cannot afford. You *can* do it, and if success is what you seek — you *will* do it.

i. Advertising

Doing business without advertising is like winking at a girl in the dark: You know what you are doing but nobody else does.

Ed Howe

Advertising can help to increase sales if it is done wisely and well. Doing it wisely means targeting your market; doing it well means placing ads that *sell*. Sounds simple enough, but like all business activities, there are tricks and traps. Advertising is a means of delivering a message. It's where and how you deliver the message that will make your advertising a positive sales force for your new business.

1. Targeting your advertising

You've spent some time analyzing your potential customers, who they are, and where they are. Use this information to find the best route to your customer. Don't scatter your advertising in publications not suitable to your market.

2. Choosing the right magazine

Start by making a visit to a well-stocked magazine store. Take your time and browse through all the publications on sale. Ask yourself the following questions:

(a) Does the magazine aim for the same market you do? You don't want to advertise in a business magazine if you are marketing baby shoes or a sports magazine if you're in the furniture repair business. That's just plain common sense. One good browse through a newsstand will quickly show you just how finely targeted today's magazines are. They spend time and money to identify their market, and that's good for you. Be sure to take advantage of it. By looking at ads and feature copy, you can readily see which publication will be right for your ad. Consider only magazines that aim directly at your customers.

(b) Does the magazine carry ads for goods or services similar to the ones you are offering? If there are no ads for products and services similar to yours, be careful. There may be a reason for it, and it might not be that you are the first one to discover the magazine. Perhaps others have tried and not been successful with the publication.

(c) Is the magazine regional or national? You do not want to pay national advertising rates if you only want to advertise in your local market. Many national magazines do have regional rates, but even these rates can be expensive. Don't overlook locally produced and distributed publications that are well circulated. They are often your best bet.

(d) Does the publication have the image you want for your business? Check the feature articles and content of the magazine to see if it fairly reflects your ideas and opinions. Consider the overall image of the magazine. If it emphasizes luxury living and your marketing strategy is to promote economy and savings, it will not be a logical choice.

When you have selected the magazines you think might be the ones for you, write to them. Ask for circulation figures and advertising prices. Most magazines keep excellent statistics on who their readers are so ask for a readership profile, too.

Another source for information on magazines is your local library. Tell the librarian what you are seeking (magazines that target seniors or vacationers, perhaps, or trade magazines that are aimed directly at selected professions and businesses), and he or she can provide you with a list of magazines that target that market. Your library can also provide you with information on rates and circulation figures for magazines as well as newspapers. In Canada, ask to see the Canadian Advertising Rates and Data (C.A.R.D.). In the United States, ask to see Standard Rates and Data Service (S.R.D.S.). Both publications are updated monthly.

3. *Your local newspaper*

Newspapers are another possible medium for your advertisement. Often the local paper is the best choice for promoting awareness of your enterprise's product or service. Newspapers are widely circulated, and it is easy to target your market by choosing the section most suitable for your ad: classifieds, entertainment, business, etc. Call and ask for advertising rates and schedules.

Classified advertising is inexpensive and widely read. Many businesses, home-based and otherwise, use this type of advertising exclusively because of its drawing power. The strong point about classified advertising is that the people who read it generally do so for a reason — they intend to buy. If you study the classified section of your local paper, you will see that some advertisements run daily, month after month. That advertiser would not put out dollars so consistently if he or she were not getting results.

If you decide to use a classified ad, be sure to choose the right section and pay particular attention to your copy. Try to make it stand out from the crowd. You can't use pictures or catchy graphics, so choose your words well and don't skimp on them. Create a good headline, and use enough copy space to sell your product or service.

4. *Flyers*

Flyers can be a useful and low budget means of getting your message to your customer. They can be produced inexpensively in large quantities, and they allow more space for you to tell your story. If the market for your product or service can be easily reached by using this type of advertising, it is well worth the effort.

While you may choose to distribute the flyers yourself, you might also consider hiring school children if the area you wish to cover is large. There are also companies that specialize in this type of distribution.

When creating your flyer, remember the image that you wish to create for your business and always emphasize the product. The rules of good advertising copy apply equally to newspapers, brochures, magazines, or flyers.

5. *Yellow Pages*

Advertising in the Yellow Pages is not cheap, but it may well be the best place to spend your advertising dollar. Directory advertising is visible for a long period of time, and it is often the first place a potential customer will look when shopping. If you can't afford a display ad, at least be certain that your business is listed.

Home business people often ignore the Yellow Pages because they are too busy trying to save a few dollars by not paying for a business phone. This can be a costly error. For a potential customer to find your business, it must be visible. Ask yourself, where do I look when I want to buy goods or services? Most probably it is your Yellow Pages. Think of all those index fingers running through those listings, day in and day out. If your company name was there, that index finger might well move from the page to the dial.

j. Making your copy sell

Your advertising budget limits the amount of space you can buy in the magazine or newspaper of your choice. That limit applies to the number of words you can use to sell your product. *Every word must count.*

Before you start to write your ad copy, take a long look at other ads that use the amount of space you plan to use. If you see a particularly good one, analyze it. Make notes on why the ad works well, and check it for key words that give the ad appeal and drawing power. Look at the layout and print selection and ask yourself if something similar would work for you. Reading and analyzing ads can help when you begin to write copy and outline a format.

Writing the ad for your business is a creative act, and, strictly speaking, there should be no shackles on that creativity. However, here are a few proven techniques that will help your ad to sell. Measure your ad against them.

(a) Advertising is a visual medium, and your ad should please the eye. Check the ad layout — does it look good? What about type — crisp and legible?

(b) It should have a good headline. Your lead phrase should capture the reader's interest, compelling him or her to read on. Your headline should offer the reader something he or she wants.

(c) It should be easy to read. Try to choose each word carefully. Does it *say* something?

(d) It should offer information in a logical sequence. Move from your headline, to copy about your product, to how and where the customer can buy it.

(e) It should be specific, not general. A good ad tells something about a product or service, not a company. Just listing your company name, address, and telephone number is not enough to pique interest in even the most curious buyer.

(f) It should appeal to the reader's self-interest. Your ad should show a benefit to the customer. It should tell why he or she should buy from you.

(g) It should be honest. Not only are there laws against misleading advertising, but dishonest advertising is also bad for business.

(h) It should have the personal touch. Think of your ad as one person talking to another. Try to make it as conversational as possible. Avoid long words or exaggerated phrases.

(i) It should stick to one main theme. Your ad copy will be more powerful if it is focused in one direction. Don't dilute your message by talking about more than one subject.

When writing your copy, think about what is unique about your product or service. Highlight that unique feature by using strong, compelling words. Good copywriting is a craft that can be learned, but it does take practice.

Reports say that the average consumer is exposed to as many as 2,000 advertising messages per day. That's a lot of competition, and it's not easy to make your ad stand out from the crowd. Despite the challenge, the power of advertising to draw customers and sell products is undisputed. For the person working from home, it can prove to be a powerful selling method.

A little research can do a lot to ensure that your advertising dollar is used to advantage. Make sure you target your advertising and monitor it. If your first ad doesn't do the job you expect, change it. Try another way to get your message across, perhaps a new layout or stronger copy. If you have chosen advertising as your main selling tool, *plan a long-term, consistent advertising program and review it often*. The effectiveness of advertising depends on constancy. It is more effective to place several well-written small ads than one large one, and often the cost is the same. It is repetition that will put your message across and build credibility for your enterprise.

k. An Internet Web site

The Internet, a global network of interconnected computers, provides still another venue to promote your business: the Web site. The Web site is a page (or pages) of information about your company and its product or service that can be created either personally — if you are Net savvy — or by a professional Web developer, who will charge a fee for services. Sites range from those using straight text to ones incorporating music, video, photographic images, and graphics.

When your Web site is built, it is uploaded to the Internet "highway" where anyone using the Net can stop by. Once there, they may read about your company and product and move on, e-mail you for more information, or place an order. The paradox of the Web site is that it needs to be promoted itself. Building it is easy; the challenge is getting it noticed. It needs the support of other media. Your Web site's Internet address, known as a URL (Uniform Resource Locator), should be prominent on all your brochures, flyers, business cards, and any other advertising you do for our company.

The other route to your site is via links to the various Internet search engines. Search programs such as AltaVista, Yahoo!, Infoseek, Webcrawler, and Lycos, given some key words, sweep the World Wide Web (WWW), identify Web sites containing those words, then list them for the surfer. If the person has keyed in words that are prominent in your site, your URL will be listed for viewing — along with hundreds of others. Most of the search programs, after asking you to read a few do's and don'ts, make linking up a simple matter.

The Internet, often described as the information highway, is not paved with gold, so don't expect overnight millions. The Net has a strong commercial presence and business is being done there, but it is not one big shopping mall with customers throwing money at every new offering. Despite this, and because business people are drawn to a potentially global market, the Web site is now a key component in most companies' promotional and marketing programs.

Don't rush headlong onto this very special "highway." A poor Web presence, over-hyped and ill-conceived, will accomplish nothing for you or your business. Do take some thoughtful steps.

Spend some time on the Internet, either with a helpful friend familiar with computers or through an Internet service provider. Check out numerous sites and try talking, via e-mail, to the site hosts. Many of them will be happy to give you tips and pointers on what

It's hard for me to get used to these changing times. I can remember when the air was clean and sex was dirty.

George Burns

Many of them will be happy to give you tips and pointers on what works or what doesn't work for them. Many homepreneurs, fearful of a technology they don't understand, ignore the Internet. I suggest you not be among them. Even if you plan to stay off the highway for now, take the time to learn about it. We approach a new millennium with lightning speed and with it comes fresh and exciting ways of connecting to potential customers. The Internet is one of them.

For more information on the Internet, check your local magazine racks. Short of being on the Net itself, magazines, with their monthly publishing schedules are your best source for current information. There are many devoted entirely to the Internet. *Internet Worlds: The Magazines for Internet Users* is one, and *NetGuide Magazine: The #1 Guide to Everything on the Net* is another. For more detailed help, check out *Doing Big Business on the Internet* by Brian Hurley and Peter Birkwood, another book in the Self-Counsel Series.

You can also call an Internet service provider. They'll be happy to answer your questions and tell you what you need in terms of hardware and software to get online. You'll find them listed under "Internet" in the Yellow Pages.

l. *Keeping a customer*

You've advertised, networked, and made some personal calls. You have devoted time, thought, and energy to getting customers. You have also spent money on the task. *The important thing now is to keep that customer.*

Selling doesn't stop the minute a customer decides to buy from you. It continues as long as you have a relationship with that customer. Selling encompasses customer relations, and that includes keeping your prices fair, standing behind your product, and providing customer service.

Success in business over the long term depends on customer loyalty. You not only want your hard-won customer to buy from you again; you also want them to speak well of your product to their friends and business associates. Let's look at a few ways to keep a customer:

(a) Follow up. Check back with your client a week or two after the sale to see how things are going and ask if he or she is satisfied.

(b) Respond to telephone calls. Don't irritate a customer by not returning calls — promptly! If you're away from your home office for long periods, check in regularly for your calls. If you use an answering machine, make sure it has a remote message system. Never make a customer wait hours or, heaven forbid, days for you to return a call.

(c) Communicate your guarantee. Let a customer know what to expect if he or she needs to return a product or has a problem with your service.

(d) Meet deadlines or delivery dates. Be organized about scheduling your time and production. Try not to disappoint a customer by delivering late.

(e) Keep your head up. Never duck a dissatisfied customer. Plan to meet customer problems head on and deal with difficulties directly and honestly.

Long-term customer relationships are built on trust and fair dealing. The successful homepreneur respects the customer and lets that respect show in every business transaction. You have asked a person to do business with you, to exchange money for goods or services. That exchange constitutes a contract, whether formal or informal. When you agree to the contract, you make a sale; when you live up to its terms and conditions, you have a customer.

When you agree to the contract, you make a sale; when you live up to its terms and conditions, you have a customer.

Let your hook always be cast; in the stream where you least expect it there will be a fish.

Ovid

THE PURPOSE OF A BUSINESS IS TO GET AND KEEP CUSTOMERS.

—*THEODORE LEVITT*

10

Managing your time

Time is the thing we have least of.

Ernest Hemingway

A businessman, walking along a beach, finds an ancient brass lamp. He gives it a light rub and a genie appears. The genie, delighted to be free, grants the man one wish. The man quickly responds, "I wish for time — all the time in the world." The genie shakes his head and answers, "You have asked me for the one thing that I cannot give. Please make another wish." The man thinks a moment and then replies, "Okay, give me the next best thing, a time management system."

It doesn't take long for the new business person to understand why the man first wished for "all the time in the world." There is never enough of this priceless commodity.

Most of us waste more time than we care to admit. We have a hard time just getting down to what needs doing — particularly if the task is large or one we won't enjoy. As demands on our time grow, we feel distress and often become disorganized. We accomplish half of what we should, fall further and further behind, and then guilt sets in. If you let it, it can be an endless circle, a wheel within a wheel. Poor use of time discourages enterprise, blocks accomplishment, and damages our self-image. It is our primary life resource, yet often we squander it. There is a saying that there are three kinds of people in the world: those who make it happen, those who watch it happen, and those who say, what happened? People who "make" it happen know the value of time.

One of the requirements for running a successful enterprise from home is practical time management. Undoubtedly, your life is already full, yet you are about to add a brand new set of responsibilities. To do justice to them, you will need to allocate and manage the time necessary. The challenge can be daunting. It will overwhelm you if you do not work out a system.

Time management is a learned skill that requires discipline and commitment. No matter how disorganized you think you are, with a little effort, you can do it. It is not without reward. Not only does it give you a feeling of control and a greater sense of accomplishment, it also helps to keep you on track.

Sensible time management begins by setting priorities.

a. Your life and time

This is the moment when most time management books tell you to get out your pencil and start making a list. I'd like to delay that process for a while. So, for the moment, put down your pencil, lean back in your chair or take a walk, then start the thinking process. Begin by reflecting on time itself:

(a) Do you believe that time is a precious, non-renewable resource?

(b) Is your time often squandered?

(c) Do you think that all your available time should be spent making money?

(d) Do you believe that time should be balanced between personal and business concerns?

(e) Is it possible to use time more effectively?

(f) Will managing your time help you achieve your goals?

(g) Can you name three things more valuable than time?

(h) What is *most important* to you?

Every person puts his or her own value on time either consciously or unconsciously. To practice sensible time management, that value must be *consciously* arrived at, analyzed, and then allocated. As you go through this chapter, please keep the things that are *most* important to you uppermost in your mind. If you don't wish to sacrifice them, allow for them in your plan. *Remember that time doing one thing is always time taken away from another.* That's why it is a good idea to assess how your time is used now before developing your time plan for your new business.

b. Where does the time go?

If you are presently working either part time or full time and are planning to start your business by working nights or weekends, this step is critical. You will have to decide what activities you will forego to make room for your new enterprise. If you are a mother with young children, for example, you already have a full schedule. You will have to organize carefully if you add yet another demanding infant, a fledgling business.

Now start to make lists, and the first will be a snapshot of your typical week. There are 168 hours in seven days and you probably sleep about 56 of them. That leaves 112 hours. What exactly do you do with those hours? Think about your time and how you spend it in an average week.

On one side of Worksheet #15, write down what you do with the time you have control over. Think of this as discretionary time, time that you make decisions about. It might be Saturday morning, or that first couple of hours after the kids have left for school. Be honest about what you do with the time you control. Do you play golf, read magazines, take a fitness class?

On the other half of the page, write down what happens that you don't control. You might call this your non-discretionary list. It will include things such as family responsibilities, car pool duties, hospital visits, or work commitments. This part of the list should also include distractions such as telephone calls or unannounced visitors.

Most distractions are time wasters only because we let them be. We blame them for all the things we don't get done. They are handy scapegoats, but taking control of them will gain you valuable time in which to conduct business.

As you do your list, try to assign a time value to each item on it. When you have done this, a clearer picture of your current use of time will emerge. Don't expect perfect accuracy. Most of us have no sure idea of where the time goes. That's the purpose of this exercise.

Once you feel comfortable with this exercise, you might wish to expand on it. Describe a typical month or year.

If this assignment leaves you at sea, try keeping a time sheet for a week or so. It's fun and can be a real eye-opener.

This is the start of sensible time management. Eventually, it will help you make decisions on how better to allocate your time.

Worksheet #15
Tracking time

In an average week, I control the following:	Time	Listed below is what I don't control:	Time
1._____	_____	1._____	_____
2._____	_____	2._____	_____
3._____	_____	3._____	_____
4._____	_____	4._____	_____
5._____	_____	5._____	_____
6._____	_____	6._____	_____
7._____	_____	7._____	_____
8._____	_____	8._____	_____
9._____	_____	9._____	_____
10._____	_____	10._____	_____
11._____	_____	11._____	_____
12._____	_____	12._____	_____
13._____	_____	13._____	_____
14._____	_____	14._____	_____
15._____	_____	15._____	_____
16._____	_____	16._____	_____
17._____	_____	17._____	_____
18._____	_____	18._____	_____
19._____	_____	19._____	_____
20._____	_____	20._____	_____

How many of the 112 hours can I account for:_____

c. *Your agenda*

Attaining goals and managing your time are inseparable. If you don't want to accomplish anything, you don't need to concern yourself with how long it will take. You can just let the days come and go and allow them to pass without thought. No planned activity is required. But if you aspire to success in your business, you have an agenda, a full agenda. Your time cannot be idle or unproductive if you want your venture to achieve its full potential.

You will have to work out just what needs to be on your agenda. For example, it should include a comprehensive list of the activities and time required to get your business up and running. You might also include the activities that will have to take place in the early days of operations.

Your agenda is your personal time plan. It will work best if you include both the business and the non-business activities that will require your time and attention. Consider your social life and time spent with your spouse, children, and friends as an essential part of your plan. Review what you have written on Worksheet #15 and allot time for activities that you cannot or choose not to sacrifice. Make time allowances for personal development, fitness, hobbies, etc.; give them the priority they deserve. Sensible time management for the homepreneur encompasses all these things. If you organize your agenda properly and make good use of time, there is no need to shortchange any of them.

d. *Planning time*

This first year of your business is a busy one. There are many steps necessary on the way to your success as a homepreneur. We have already discussed many of them, such as organizing your work space, planning your sales strategy, getting your business license, registering your name, and so on. The list is a long one, and as you begin to receive orders for goods, deal with suppliers, keep books and records, etc., demands for your time escalate. Pressures other than those you put on yourself take more and more of your time.

It's a good idea to organize your agenda from the very beginning. It helps to divide it into three segments: long term, intermediate, and immediate. Define each segment of time in whatever way you like.

For example, long-term agenda could be a year or it could be six months if you find that time frame works better for you.

1. *The long-term agenda*

The foundation of time management is list making — setting down what you are going to do and when you plan to do it. Begin by deciding how long your long term is to be, and then make a list of activities required in that time period. Using Worksheet #16, describe the activity, estimate the time it will take, and then give it a priority rank: 1, 2, 3, etc. Don't try to rank the activities as you write them down. You will find that assigning priority takes some thought, and it is easier to list what has to be done first and worry about ranking later. The main purpose of this agenda is to consider every possibility. Make the list as complete as you can.

2. *The intermediate agenda*

Your long-term agenda likely runs to more than one page if it is as complete as it should be. You begin to refine your agenda when you do the intermediate section. Start by reviewing every item on the long-term list. If you have chosen six months as your intermediate period, transfer all the things that need to be accomplished in this time frame to the new list.

Use Worksheet #17 to prepare your intermediate agenda. Cross items off the long-term agenda as you enter them on your intermediate agenda. On the intermediate agenda, you will also set priorities, and you will set specific dates for completion. Again, do not try to write the list in rank order. Enter the planned activity, then assign a rank number.

3. *The immediate agenda*

Use Worksheet #18 to create your immediate agenda. Follow the same procedure you used above. Scan the date column of the intermediate list and transfer all activities that require prompt attention to the new list. If you have designated one week as the time period of your immediate agenda, look for dates that fall within that period. Write all the activities for that time span on the new list. Enter them in order of date. If you wish, you can bypass the immediate agenda and enter your planned activities in your business diary. If you do this, don't forget to estimate the allocated time.

Worksheet #16
Long-term agenda

List of activities to be complete by: _____
                                     mo.   day   yr.

Priority rank	Activity to complete	Estimated time
_____	_____	_____
_____	_____	_____
_____	_____	_____
_____	_____	_____
_____	_____	_____
_____	_____	_____
_____	_____	_____
_____	_____	_____
_____	_____	_____
_____	_____	_____
_____	_____	_____
_____	_____	_____
_____	_____	_____
_____	_____	_____
_____	_____	_____
	TOTAL TIME	_____

Worksheet #17
Intermediate agenda

Time period from_____to_____
                        mo.   day   yr.   mo.   day   yr.

Priority rank	Activity to complete	Estimated time	Completion date
_____	_____	_____	_____
_____	_____	_____	_____
_____	_____	_____	_____
_____	_____	_____	_____
_____	_____	_____	_____
_____	_____	_____	_____
_____	_____	_____	_____
_____	_____	_____	_____
_____	_____	_____	_____
_____	_____	_____	_____
_____	_____	_____	_____
_____	_____	_____	_____

TOTAL TIME _____

Worksheet #18
Immediate agenda

Time period from_____to_____
                mo.   day   yr.   mo.   day   yr.

Date to complete	Description of activity	Estimated time	Done?
_____	_____	_____	_____
_____	_____	_____	_____
_____	_____	_____	_____
_____	_____	_____	_____
_____	_____	_____	_____
_____	_____	_____	_____
_____	_____	_____	_____
_____	_____	_____	_____
_____	_____	_____	_____
_____	_____	_____	_____
_____	_____	_____	_____
_____	_____	_____	_____
_____	_____	_____	_____
_____	_____	_____	_____

e. More tips on time management

By developing a time-management system, you are taking control of the events that influence the quality of your working life. Here are a few tips, most of them from other homepreneurs, that might help.

- Be a list maker. List making helps keep you focused and is a surefire aid to memory. Avoid making multiple lists though. Organize your time from a central list and keep it with your time-management calender. A hard-bound, plain lined notebook that will act as a master list is a good idea. It will stay neat and last for several months.

- Think of action in a time perspective. When you put an item on the list, always estimate how long it will take. While this may seem difficult at first, with time and practice it quickly becomes second nature. Don't forget to include travel time for appointments away from your office — it's a real time user.

- Prioritize your responsibilities. You will accomplish more if you are systematic in your approach. By ranking the activities, you can exercise greater control over your working day. Setting priorities and working methodically goes a long way to keeping stressful situations to the minimum.

- Make sure your time-management system is portable. Keep it with you always, and refer to it often. Keeping your plans and schedule in one place is a great time saver. Try to avoid accumulating little scraps of paper with important notes on them. If you make such notes, write them on adhesive notepaper then attach them to the appropriate page in your planning diary. Later, take a moment or two to rewrite the information in your system.

- Avoid time wasters and distractions. When you have planned your time for the day or week, don't let personal telephone calls or visitors take you from your

YOU WILL NEVER FIND TIME FOR ANYTHING. IF YOU WANT TIME, YOU HAVE TO MAKE IT.

—CHARLES BUSTON

purpose. Learn to deal with them courteously and effectively. This will come easier to you as your business grows, but a firm approach to time wasters is a necessity.

- Keep your work organized. Don't have a desk or work area that looks as though it has been buffeted by a strong wind. Clean off your desk every night before you leave it. And don't forget to use your garbage can! If something has been sitting on your desk for six weeks and you still haven't acted on it, you probably never will. File it or dispose of it.

- Develop a filing system and stick to it. Pay particular attention to telephone messages and notes. Have a specific place for them on your desk. If you don't file every day, at least make time for it once a week. Between times keep a "TO BE FILED" file and *don't put it out of sight*. To be safe, put the filing activity on your list and prioritize it.

- Don't be a keeper. You already receive a lot of mail, and you will get even more when you are in business. Be ruthless with unwanted mail. You don't need junk mail cluttering up your desk. There's only one place for unwanted paper — your recycling bin. Ditto with magazines. If a magazine contains an article you intend to read, tear it out and save it for later. No need to heap your office with bulky magazines that are 90% advertising.

- Give time to time. Review your plan daily. Take the first few minutes of each day to look over your plan. This rule is sacrosanct to sensible time management. Give your time the respect it deserves and allow an hour or so to plan, organize, and review.

f. Family, friends, and time

A real test for the homepreneur's time-management system can be the people they care about most: family and friends. If it is their custom to telephone or drop in unexpectedly, ask for their support in changing that habit. With a little diplomacy, this can be done.

The difficulty with friends and family is that while they might agree and express understanding about your new responsibilities, they often think that you don't truly mean it, or, at least, you don't mean *them*. It may take more than one request before they take your business as seriously as you do.

One of the best ways to deter unwanted visitors and telephone calls is to establish a working routine and stick to it. Make that routine known to the people likely to follow the old pattern of dropping by. Your new status as home business person will be respected if you tell family and friends when you will be working and when you will not. They are more likely to be accommodating if they have some idea of your schedule. The secret is to tell family and friends *in advance* about your new situation and not to alienate them with repeated and easily misunderstood rejections such as "I can't talk now, I'm really busy," or a brusque, "I'll call you later."

While many homepreneurs are successful in orienting friends and adult family members to their new status, children can prove more challenging. For very young children, you may need to arrange child care for at least part of your work time (see chapter 2) as they are not inclined to respect the importance of that production deadline or pivotal customer meeting. Older children, however, can be influenced by visual confirmation that you are indeed working and unavailable except in case of an emergency. This may mean dressing for work in a consistent manner — a business suit, for instance. Help the older child understand that when you are dressed in such a way you are "at work" and can't be disturbed. The mode of dress acts as a visual reminder of the new rules. One home-based accountant with teenage children had a sign made for her office door, "Brain Surgery in Progress. Do not disturb!" The kids were made to understand that when that sign was up, it had to be very serious indeed before any interruption was tolerated.

There is no reason that your new venture should cost you the love and companionship of people who matter to you. If you are honest about what you are doing and manage your time properly, such relationships need not end, but simply change a little to accommodate your new enterprise.

g. *Time-management systems*

Walk into any office stationery shop and you will find a selection of calendars, diaries, and time-management systems. All are designed to help you get and stay organized. They range in price from a few dollars for a vinyl-covered diary to a hundred dollars or more for a fully expanded time-management system complete with all accessories. Such accessories include things such as appointment calendars,

The Bird of Time has but a little way to flutter — and the Bird is on the wing.

Omar Khayyam

143

meeting schedules, customer call sheets, expense sheets, and automobile mileage records.

If you are a computer user, there are some excellent systems available that offer calendars, memo capability, and extensive list-making facilities. While the computer itself is not portable, unless it is a laptop type, day sheets and plans can be printed for your convenience. One of the good things about computerized systems is that they don't let you forget. Once you enter an item on your "things to do" list, the computer will automatically carry the item forward until you indicate that it is done.

A computerized system, like any other, is only valuable if you use it consistently. While I would not recommend the purchase of an expensive computer purely to manage your time, it is a definite option when a computer is justified by other business considerations.

Whatever time management system you choose, either one you develop on your own or a ready-made one, use it regularly. Taking the time to plan and monitor your activities is central to time management — and a successful enterprise. For more information on time management, you might want to read *Making Time Work for You* by Harold L. Taylor (see Appendix 2) and *No B.S. Time Management for Entrepreneurs* by Dan Kennedy, another title in the Self-Counsel Series.

11

Business technology

Man is a tool-using animal....Without tools he is nothing, with tools he is all.

Thomas Carlyle

Modern technology provides a glittering array of new tools, all intended to make running a business easier and more efficient. The selection of products and systems is so extensive that it can be intimidating to the new homepreneur. The vocabulary is confusing, too. It talks about bits, bytes, modems, baud rates, and interfaces, when all you want to know is what it can do for your business. You might worry that the cost is too high and ask yourself, "Is all this razzle-dazzle worth it?" You might even be a little fearful if you have never before worked with computers or other high-tech equipment. On the flip side of the coin are the people who can't wait to install and use as much technology as possible. To them the computer, cellular phone, and fax machine are status symbols. They often talk more about the technology they use than the business they're in. Both attitudes, rush and reticence, can be damaging to the start-up enterprise.

The first year of your business may not be the time to buy high-tech equipment, but it is the time to start thinking about it. There are many things to learn as you work through the first 12 months and one is the benefits of technology. If you decide you don't want a computer, or that owning a fax has no advantages for your operation, that's fine. Just try to make sure that the decision is an informed one. Start the learning process early and position yourself to make a decision that will be good for your business.

Let's start by looking at that old standby of the small business person, the personal computer (PC). Yes, I did say old. The first PC was used in scientific laboratories in the early 1970s. Now with installations numbering in the millions, it is a proven and dependable business tool.

a. Do you need a computer?

One machine can do the work of fifty ordinary men. No machine can do the work of one extraordinary man.

Elbert Hubbard

Sooner or later the home-based business person is going to think about owning and using a computer. Chances are it will be a PC, a microcomputer capable of business applications. The decision will involve purchasing hardware (the physical equipment and components) and software (the set of programmed instructions that tell the computer what to do). The choices for each seem endless. Fortunately, there is also a lot of information available to help you make the decision. To their credit, manufacturers of both hardware and software have devoted a lot of effort to creating user-friendly products.

Despite the manufacturer's efforts, you may still feel perplexed when you try to decide whether to purchase your first computer. You might well wonder how you will know if you need something if you don't know what it does. The trick is not to think about what the computer will do but rather what *you* will be doing. Once your tasks are identified, the next step is to decide if the computer can help. Chances are, if the task is repetitive and clerical in nature, it can. Most homepreneurs take their first tentative step toward technology when they realize they can use a computer for correspondence or basic file management.

But the computer is also a creative tool. Beginning users are almost always surprised by the creativity that is unleashed as knowledge and confidence grow. They may start out doing a few letters, but in a short time they are producing ad pieces, proposals, and reports with flair and élan.

Think again about the three-legged stool analogy I used earlier: administration, finance, and marketing. The computer has something to offer to each of them. On Worksheet #19, check off the jobs that need to be done in your business and indicate how many times in each month they will be required. If you can think of other things that will take up your time and might benefit from a computer, write them down. Don't concern yourself with the question marks. We'll go back to them later, after we've had a quick review of computer applications.

When you think about computers, keep your eye fixed on your business needs. If you know what you want it to do before you start the selection process, your job will be easier. Remember that computers perform a variety of tasks well so don't limit yourself. It is more easily cost justified if it serves more than one need.

b. Computer applications

Computers are used for a variety of purposes and each use is called an "application." Many applications are highly specialized, such as weather forecasting or electronic funds transfer. They have been developed over time, at great cost, to fit the needs of a particular market.

What follows is a look at the main computer applications useful to the small business person and a short list of software programs available to run them. (Such programs are also called packages.) While the programs mentioned below are well-known and respected, they are only the tip of a very large and constantly growing iceberg. There are hundreds, perhaps thousands, of competing ones, and many of them are excellent. New ones come on the market at a furious pace, and even experts are challenged to give an informed opinion on their individual merits. It doesn't help that unbiased opinions from users are hard to find. When it comes to software, everyone loves — and swears by — the package they use, undoubtedly because they invested so much time and effort getting proficient at it. It is not unusual to find a dedicated fan of a particular word processing program declaring with conviction that it is the finest package on the market without ever having tried another.

The software products that I mention are distributed widely and well supported. Some of them, such as Microsoft Word, Corel's WordPerfect, Lotus 1-2-3, and Ventura, have set the standards for the industry. The advantage of choosing widely used software is that there is a lot of help available and when you are just learning about computers or a particular program, that help is invaluable.

After you've read through the list, go back to Worksheet #19 and, under the question marks, make a note of the application that could help you: accounting, word processing, etc.

Most small business people buy their programs off the shelf at a local computer store. You can also purchase through mail order, or if you're technically able, through the machine itself via modem at online computer malls. An established store is a good place to start if you are new to the world of computers and software.

Worksheet #19
Determining possible computer uses for your business

ADMINISTRATION	YES/NO	HOW OFTEN	???
Production schedules	_____	_____	_____
Letters	_____	_____	_____
Personnel	_____	_____	_____
Inventory	_____	_____	_____
Reminders	_____	_____	_____
Client files	_____	_____	_____

FINANCIAL:

Cash flow planning	_____	_____	_____
Budgets	_____	_____	_____
Accounting	_____	_____	_____
Tax planning	_____	_____	_____
Customer billing	_____	_____	_____

MARKETING:

Presentations	_____	_____	_____
Mailing lists	_____	_____	_____
Brochures	_____	_____	_____
Proposals	_____	_____	_____
Sales letters	_____	_____	_____
Sales reports	_____	_____	_____

OTHER:

_____	_____	_____	_____

Don't even think of buying on your first time out. Just plan to browse and ask some questions. Be straightforward, and tell the salesperson that you are doing some research on programs that might be good for your business. It must be said that not all computer salespeople in the stores are as knowledgeable as they could be about the products they sell. This can leave a nervous new buyer in a quandary. It might help to ask friends or business associates where they bought their computer products. Ask them for the name of an informed sales representative, and find out about the after-sales support offered by the store. A solid referral will make your task simpler.

Salespeople who are good at their job will ask you questions about what you do. They want some idea of what your needs will be. If your salesperson doesn't question you, head for another store.

1. *Accounting*

Accounting software provides general ledger, accounts receivable, payable, and invoicing. It also will print monthly statements for all your accounts. Many programs have job costing and payroll modules. They also print monthly statements and payroll checks, although this application is not much use to a one- or two-person operation.

A good accounting package will give you an accounts receivable list every month or more often if you would like. It will also tell you who owes you, how much they owe you, and if the money is overdue and by how many days. Such a list is valuable both for analysis and collection efforts. Generally such lists "age" your receivables by placing them in columns labeled 30, 60, 90, and 120 days. If an amount is in the 60-day column, for example, you know the amount is 60 days overdue.

The invoicing portion of such programs generally provides a crisp, professional bill for presentation to your customer. Many of these packages provide some inventory control functions as well. Software packages to consider are the following:

    (a) ACC-PAC

    (b) M.Y.O.B.

    (c) Simply Accounting

    (d) Quickbooks

2. *Word processing*

Word processing (WP) allows you to enter and revise written information with ease and flexibility. You can use it for letters, typing your invoices (if you don't use an accounting package), maintaining a mailing list, and any other writing jobs that your business demands. One other plus for WP is that the best packages have both a spelling checker and thesaurus built in — a great help if you're nervous about your writing skills. Some of the better WP programs incorporate basic desktop publishing features that can help orient you to the larger more powerful programs.

Some popular WP programs are —

(a) Microsoft Word

(b) Corel WordPerfect, and

(c) Lotus Word Pro.

The fight continues between WordPerfect and Microsoft Word for first place in the market. Both programs are first rate, and both offer more features than you might use in a lifetime.

3. *Spreadsheets*

A spreadsheet is the computerized version of the column pad. In grid fashion, it is divided into rows and columns. Where the row and column meet on the screen is called a cell. When you have entered information in the cells (e.g., sales and expenses), you tell the computer what to do by using a few keystrokes. The keystrokes cause the computer to add, subtract, divide, etc., and then calculate the answer for you.

Spreadsheets are used extensively in forecasting, budgeting, and general business planning. The ability to enter changes and update a cash flow or sales forecast almost effortlessly simplifies what can be a time-consuming task. Popular spreadsheet software programs are —

(a) Borland Quattro Pro

(b) Lotus 1•2•3

(c) Microsoft Excel

4. *Desktop publishing*

Desktop publishing (DTP) is software that enables the user to combine text, drawings, and graphics to produce publishable material. Using DTP, you could, for example, produce a camera-ready brochure or newsletter containing various sizes and types of print that look professionally typeset. DTP allows you to do most of the work previously done by a professional typesetter. Sounds good, but the problem is that advanced DTP programs require expensive hardware, such as graphic monitors and laser printers. Such hardware is not easy to justify in a new home-based business, unless, of course, DTP is your business. Examples of these high-end programs for the sophisticated user are Corel Ventura and Pagemaker.

Some smaller, less expensive programs that will give you some of the benefits of DTP without the costs are Microsoft Publisher and The Print Shop. These programs will enable you to create mailers and flyers at a fraction of the cost of the full-blown DTP program and without major hardware investment. And don't overlook the *publishing* potential in your word processing programs. Versatile word processing programs, such as Corel WordPerfect and Microsoft Word may give you all the DTP capacity needs.

5. *Data base management*

The objective of data base management (DBM) is to allow the user to store and retrieve information. You set your records up and define the information in the way that works best for you. Information, once entered, can be called up on your screen at any time through a simple search process. You can then update, delete, change, or modify it in any way you like. Examples of data base applications include inventory management, telephone directories, client files, mailing lists, and customized order processing.

If your business requires that you work consistently with large amounts of information that must be classified, modified, or updated, you may want to consider a data base program. Programs to consider for data base management are —

(a) Borland Paradox

(b) Lotus Approach

(c) Microsoft Access

(d) dBase for Windows

Other software packages include things such as business planning, built-in calculators, time-management systems, time-billing systems, appointment calendars, and graphics packages. You can even find programs that will check your grammar and suggest ways to improve your writing. Many of them are useful for helping the business person get, and stay, organized.

c. Choosing software

It can be tough for a new user to judge what is good software and what isn't. By good I mean easy to learn and use while still being powerful enough to meet your business needs. You can make the job of evaluating software less error prone if you follow these steps before making any purchase:

(a) Take a course. Nothing beats education as a route to confidence building, and courses offering computer and software training abound. Many of the courses are in seminar format and provide a lot of information in a short period of time. If you are completely new to computers, think about taking an introductory course. If you have a working knowledge of them already and know what software you want to use, attend a course developed for the program of your choice. The important thing to remember in both cases is that you do not have to know everything about a computer's innards to use one productively in your business. The basics are enough.

(b) Ask around. If you plan to buy accounting software, check with your accountant. Accountants have worked with the output of many accounting packages and can give helpful advice based on practical experience. If you have customers who use computers, check with them about what software they use.

(c) Check the manual that comes with the software. Good documentation is a sign of good software. Check to see if the manual that comes with your software is well organized and readable.

Don't let the size of the manual put you off. Some software vendors produce guides that rival the New York City telephone book in pure bulk. Don't worry about it. You don't have to read every single line to make the software run. Most well-written manuals should have you using the software after reading the first few pages.

Remember to ask if there is a telephone support number. Service-oriented software manufacturers often offer a toll-free number that you can call to get help when you need it.

(d) Make sure the program has a learning module. A learning section in the program takes you through the system step by step. It allows you to "play" with the software until you feel at ease with it.

For example, if you buy an accounting package, the learning module might ask you to set up a make-believe company. It will explain each entry you make as you go through the module and why you are making it. The great thing about learning on a computer is that you can repeat a step over and over again until you get it right. You can learn at your own pace and without pressure.

(e) Ask if the program has online help. Most software packages come with an online help system as part of the program. When you run into trouble, you hit a specified key and receive instructions. This feature serves the inexperienced user well. Between a good manual and online help, most learning problems are readily overcome.

(f) Make sure the demonstration is adequate. You should develop at least a basic understanding of the software from the salesperson's demonstration. Ask every question that comes to mind. Don't be shy. Don't expect to grasp all the fine points of the program in one showing, but you should understand enough to purchase with confidence.

(g) Know someone you can call for help. Again, it is very helpful if you have a friend or associate who has some experience with computers and the software package that you choose. No matter how helpful the manual and how available the online help facility, you will probably still have times when you're just plain stumped. It happens to everybody; it's not the end of the world. Having someone to call can save time during the learning process.

If no one you know works with computers, check the classifieds. Many home-based consulting businesses can lend some support for a reasonable price.

(h) Read. Many magazines on the newsstands are dedicated to the computer user. While some of them are so technical they're unintelligible to most of us mere mortals, others provide useful, understandable information, even for the relative beginner. A couple of useful ones offering accessible information are *PC Novice* and *Home Office Computing*. Both are monthly publications and both are widely available.

Watch for the issues that rate software for ease of use and feature comparisons. General business magazines also carry articles on computers and software. Often the information is not as technical.

Don't be tempted to use illegally copied software for your business applications. *Copying software is illegal.* It is an infringement of the producer's copyright. By using pirated software you condone an illegal practice. Sure, the price is right — nothing. But nothing can be what you get. By using pirated software, you do not have the benefit of the manufacturer's support through documentation or telephone hotline. You should realize, too, that manufacturers of software are constantly updating their products. New versions can come out as often as once a year. Usually, special discount prices are offered to registered users for the purchase of the most current version.

d. Computer hardware

Before you can run the software you have chosen, you will need to buy the hardware or physical equipment. While you don't need to spend a fortune on hardware, don't make the mistake of underbuying. You will want a machine that meets your needs today and is easily upgraded and expanded for the future. If you plan to expand your business, add more software applications, or use your computer for extensive record keeping, make your purchase with this in mind. A computer is a set of hardware components; try to evaluate each of them independently before you make your purchase.

Take one step into the market for a computer and you will be faced with the question, do I buy an IBM, an Apple, or a clone? There is no easy answer because they all have something to offer.

Generally speaking, there are two types of computers to choose from: IBM (or a compatible) or the Apple. While the large software companies offer product for both, many small and innovative software manufacturers concentrate on developing software for IBM/compatibles only, the dominant force in business computing. Whether you choose an Apple computer or an IBM/compatible, standard wisdom says you should choose your software first — then choose the best computer to run it on.

Computer manufacturers no doubt hate this advice, but it is still the recommended path for the neophyte's first step into computers. It is much easier to judge what you want to get out of the computer than what a manufacturer decides to put into it. If you do choose an IBM compatible, check out the manufacturer's history of service and reliability. Not all computers are built to the highest standards; don't let price alone be your guide. A cheap IBM compatible may be just that — cheap, a patchwork of electronics that is as trustworthy as a leaky canoe. By using a reputable computer dealer who offers support — and a solid warranty — you needn't buy now and regret later. Some respected IBM compatible computers are —

(a) Hewlett-Packard

(b) Dell

(c) Compaq

Here is a brief look at the various parts of a computer with some suggestions about what you need to start thinking about.

1. Microprocessor

The microprocessor is the integrated circuit, the brain, of the computer. It is where, if you cared to look, you would see the microchips that control the computer. Most of these chips are numbered, and the numbers, until Intel switched to calling their latest microchip the Pentium, show the evolution of the speed and processing capability of the microprocessor: 286, 386, 486, etc. Microchip manufacturers continually work to improve and refine their product to offer greater reliability and blazing processing speed.

Do you care? Yes, because you don't want a slow machine. Speed is measured in megahertz (Mhz). One megahertz equals one million cycles per second. While just a few short years ago, computers boasted speeds as low as 8 and 16 Mhz, today 200 and up is considered standard with a tripling of that speed on the near horizon. To the new computer user, hesitant and unsure, even the slowest computer can seem fast. But as expertise grows, patience ebbs, and those megahertz become increasingly important. If you foresee that your business will demand your spending many hours at the computer, you'd be wise to buy the fastest machine you can afford.

2. Random access memory (RAM)

RAM is primary storage. It is used by the operating system, the applications programs, and the data being processed. Data and instructions flow in and out of it as operations are performed. When you turn off the machine, most of what is in this memory is erased. Think of it as your computer's short-term working memory. The sophisticated programs in use today often require a great deal of RAM. Critical technical people go so far as to label some of them "memory hogs." Today, memory is most often purchased by the megabyte, with one megabyte (MB) representing approximately a million characters.

Your concern with RAM is to ensure that you have enough to run the programs you select. It's easy to see that it won't do you any good to bring home a series of programs needing 32 megabytes when your computer is equipped with 8. The good news is that the memory requirements of software are clearly indicated on the packaging, and more memory can be added later if you need it.

3. *Disk storage*

Disk storage is the secondary memory of your computer — the long-term memory. It is here that your programs and data are retained on a permanent basis, going back and forth between RAM and your disk as you work. When you exit your computer properly, all data remains on disk.

The disk size you need depends on the memory requirements of the programs you'll use and the amount of data you'll be storing on the disk. Don't worry, it's not necessary to make intricately detailed calculations before buying. Disk storage of well over 100 megabytes is common on most of today's computers, and it is usually more than enough to handle home business volumes. While you can add more disk space later, the cost of disk storage is reasonable, and it's a good idea not to shortchange yourself when you make your original purchase.

4. *Screen*

It is your screen (or monitor) that lets you see what is going on within your computer. It is the visible link, and, along with the keyboard, the hardware component that you will use most directly. Spend some time taking a good look at the wide selection of monitors now available. A poor screen can get very tiresome if you spend even a few hours with it, so choose carefully. Monitors come in varying sizes, ranging from 14 to over 20 inches, and generally offer full color. A 14-inch monitor is more than adequate for most computing tasks and is the least expensive. But if you plan to use your computer for extensive graphics, you'll want to investigate the large monitor — although those extra inches will eat a hole in your budget.

5. *Keyboard*

Some keyboards can be very frustrating to people capable of high-speed touch-typing. Any salesperson will let you type for a while so that you can get the feel of a keyboard. Try before you buy.

6. *Printer*

Printers are as abundant as computers. The three main types are laser, dot matrix, and ink jet.

The dot matrix is widely used with personal computers. This type of printer creates characters by using dot combinations created by a series of pins. Printers with the greatest number of pins produce the highest quality of print. Dot matrix printers function in two modes: draft, which gives a quick, though not letter-quality, printout, and near letter-quality (NLQ). The NLQ function of the newer dot matrix printers is excellent, looking much like text produced on a top-grade typewriter. This printer allows you to use various print sizes and types within a document, offering needed versatility to the small business person. It can also print low-quality graphics, which can be handy for sales material.

The other type of printer is the laser, the printer of choice for the business person who demands consistently crisp, high-quality texts and images for his or her business. In fact, the type and graphics produced on a good laser printer are of such sharp definition the user can, if he or she chooses, bypass typesetting completely. The laser printer is more expensive than the dot matrix, but prices are coming down. In most cases a home business can justify acquiring a laser printer only if the business is dealing with high-volume text and graphics.

Smaller, cheaper, and capable of many of the tasks performed by the laser, the ink jet printer is another workable possibility for the home business. Many homepreneurs find this printer provides them with greater flexibility and speed than the dot matrix while at the same time giving them some of the sharp graphics capability of the laser.

7. *Mouse*

A mouse is a hand-sized device attached to a computer by a wire. It functions as pointer and controls the screen cursor, the small flashing light on your screen that tells you where you are. You place the mouse on an even surface beside your computer and move it over an area approximately the size of your screen. As you move it, the cursor on your screen moves in the same direction. When you decide what you want the computer to do, you move the cursor to the appropriate place on the screen and push a button on the mouse. The computer then executes that function, storing your text, opening a new file, or whatever.

A mouse not only saves keystrokes, but also helps the inexperienced typist get around the screen quickly and accurately. A mouse allows you to make task selections from a software menu, give system commands, draw, edit, and work with graphics. Perhaps just a helpful accessory for the proficient user of some software packages such as word processing or accounting, it is essential for more creative work such as desktop publishing or drawing. If you buy an Apple computer, you will be working with a mouse. Apple can take most of the credit for the mouse's popularity as its system command structure is based on the use of a mouse.

e. *The two biggest mistakes you can make*

The two worst mistakes you can make with computers and software are an uninformed purchase and an uninformed rejection.

Is the computer a requirement for every business? Perhaps not. Businesses can be too small to support the cost. If, for example, you have half a dozen customers and only a few accounting entries a month, you don't need a computer to handle your accounting. A simple ledger is adequate.

On the other hand, if you are an aggressive marketer with plans to add one or two customers a month, you may not want to be without word processing software. Its ability to maintain your mailing list and print those good-looking sales letters will be a real boon.

The sale of computers to home-based business is on the rise. Studies now show that over 50% of businesses run from the home use computers. While many business operators stick to basic word processing and spreadsheets, others are finding new and innovative ways to use this new partner and ally. They are purchasing and using file-management systems and extensive mail programs to help them market their service or product. One home operator I spoke to called her computer a private secretary. "He keeps me organized," she said, "and no matter what the cost of living index is I don't have to give him a raise every year."

The professional homepreneur needs to be aware of tools that will make the business more efficient.

The professional homepreneur needs to be aware of tools that will make the business more efficient. Often the computer is exactly the right tool.

f. Computer comfort

You will be spending many hours with your computer, particularly through the learning phase. The experience of working with a keyboard and screen can be tiring and unenjoyable unless you set your computer up so that you are comfortable. Your back and your eyes will be grateful if you do. There is no reason not to be at ease and relaxed when you work with your system. Just ensure the following:

(a) Make sure that the chair you sit in is adjustable for seat height, and that it is on castors that roll easily. If your work area is carpeted, you might consider a piece of hard plastic for the chair area or special castors for use on carpet. The chair back should be adjustable and offer firm support to the lower back area. Your comfort will depend on whether you can shift your body and change positions easily.

(b) The keyboard should be a couple of inches lower than standard desk height to allow your hands to be at approximately the same angle as your elbows. If you cannot afford a proper computer desk to start with, check a computer supply store for an attachable, pullout tray for your keyboard. They are inexpensive, and they fasten easily under existing counters and desks.

(c) If you are keying from copy, use a copy holder. Upright copy at about the same eye level as your screen saves your eyes from having to constantly refocus.

(d) Place your screen to minimize glare and avoid light reflection from other parts of the room. It is irritating and contributes to eye strain if you see reflected images on your monitor. To avoid this, you may want to have less light in the room when you work with your computer. A dimmer switch might be a good investment.

(e) If your eyes are very sensitive, try using a non-glare screen shield. These devices go over the face of your computer monitor and cut monitor glare without impeding your vision. They are easily attached and can be purchased at most computer supply stores.

(f) Remember to get up and stretch occasionally. Sitting for long periods of time is not good for your circulation and can cause muscle cramps. By just standing up and walking around for a few minutes every hour or so, this problem is easily eliminated.

g. *Facsimile machines*

Facsimile processing machines (FAX) are a convenient and widely used means of communications and have proved to a valuable asset to the home-based business person. Most can't do without it.

From the user's point of view, FAX technology is uncomplicated and versatile. You place the document you want transmitted into your machine, dial the receiving FAX number, and away it goes. The equipment converts the information into a machine-readable format and sends it through standard telephone lines.

Because of its wide acceptance in the commercial marketplace, FAX is becoming more affordable every day. At the low end, a basic machine can be had for under $500. If you sell your product or service to other businesses, they will probably be asking for your FAX number before long. Speed, accuracy, and efficiency are just some of the benefits that have helped to make FAX standard equipment in homes and offices across North America. Your letter, order, proposal, quotation, or information request is received immediately. Your message is accurate. There is no room for error or misunderstandings. Unlike an order placed or received over the telephone, where important information can be lost or misunderstood, FAX provides both parties with a written record of the transaction. It also eliminates having to play telephone tag. Anyone in business soon knows the frustration of trying to reach a busy customer or supplier over the telephone. Hours, and sometimes even days, can be lost as each party vainly tries to connect with the other to pass along valuable information. Using FAX, this problem need not exist.

Because of the speed and reliability of FAX communication, it is used for much more than routine correspondence. Consider the following applications:

(a) More and more businesses are placing orders for supplies and services by FAX. They are not only saving time, they are ensuring that the items and quantities ordered and the scheduled delivery date are communicated accurately and completely. Even small delis and sandwich shops have installed FAX to take lunch orders from on-the-run workers in downtown office towers.

(b) Many companies are now putting out bids and quotations to potential suppliers through their FAX machines. They outline the needs and specifications in the FAX tender and request prices.

(c) You can use a FAX to request information. This is the step before purchase, when a potential customer asks questions about a possible supplier. Using FAX is an efficient way of gathering information or doing market research for future reference.

FAX machines have several options that might be of value to your business. Additional features will cost you more, but depending on your need and budget, some of them may be helpful.

(a) Auto-dialling: The same feature that is available on a telephone system allows you to record and store your most frequently called number.

(b) Delayed transmission: This feature can save you money if you are sending information long distance. It allows you to transmit outside normal business hours when rates are their lowest.

(c) Copying: Some FAX machines have a built-in photocopy capability. The quality of the copy is not as good as that of a full copy machine, but it is adequate if your copying needs are small.

(d) Telephone and answering function: Many FAX machines offer voice communication and document transmission. They can also be equipped with a telephone answering machine.

(e) Forward dialling: Some FAX machines have the ability to send messages to another machine if the first number is busy or cannot be reached.

(f) Confidential password: This is a new feature designed to eliminate junk FAX. Unless the sender uses your password, your machine will not receive the transmission.

h. Do you need fax?

One of the fundamentals of business is information exchange. Rapid, sure communication of important letters, quotes, specifications, orders, contracts, and reports can be critical to winning sales and maintaining customer service. FAX helps business people to do just that. You will know that you need FAX when —

(a) you are using courier and messenger services to deliver information several times a month. Delivery is expensive, so keep careful records from the very beginning of your business.

(b) all your customers use FAX routinely. If most of your customers are FAX users, you may find it necessary to install your own as a way of ensuring good service.

(c) you need information fast. Waiting for that order, request, or proposal can get frustrating when you know you could get it by FAX instantly.

(d) your competitors use FAX. If you see FAX used to advantage by your competitors, it may be time for one of your own.

If you are uncertain FAX is necessary for your business, you might consider using a service. A FAX service will let you send and receive messages for a few dollars a page. Check for one close to your home. Some of the efficiencies of facsimile processing will be lost if you have to drive halfway across town to pick up or send messages.

i. Telephone

Of all the technology available to the home-based business person, none is more critical than the telephone. The telephone has been around so long that we take it for granted. It's there. It works. What else is there? People who work from home know that the telephone is their business lifeline. Many homepreneurs conduct 90% of their business by phone. Hands down, it is your single most important business tool.

Telephones offer many features that are of great benefit to the home-based business person. So before you buy and install your new phone, review these features and choose a phone that will be a real helpmate. Think about the following options:

(a) Auto dialling: One-touch dialling for frequently called numbers is not only convenient, it saves time.

(b) Call forwarding: With this feature, you're not chained to the phone. You can be sure that important call will get to you no matter where you are.

(c) Call waiting: This feature is indispensable if you are on the phone for long periods. A small tone lets you know that someone, a valued customer perhaps, is trying to get through. You can momentarily interrupt the call you're on and respond. That's good business and good sales technique. If you do choose this feature, be sure you give the first call priority. You will be sure to irritate the original caller if you interrupt and put him or her on a long hold.

(d) Speaker phone: Speaker phone capability is convenient if more than one person needs the details given over the phone. This feature can also be a real boon if you need your hands to search for reference material or to make notes.

(e) Redial: Another little time saver, particularly for numbers not on your auto dial.

(f) Cordless: A cordless telephone lets you move freely about your home and still answer your phone promptly. If you're not a desk sitter, this may be the one feature you must have.

(g) Voice mail: If you can't answer your phone, your telephone company will, by taking and storing messages from callers that you can't get to because, either you're not in or you're already on the phone. With voice mail there are no busy signals; it answers instantly. Just a friendly message — in your voice — telling the caller you'll get back to him or her as quickly as possible. Combined with call waiting, this option ensures your customer's call will be treated with respect. It also provides him or her with the option of reviewing and rewording the intended message.

j. Answering machines

If you're monitoring those overheads — and you should be — you might prefer paying a one-time charge for an answering machine rather than the monthly costs of voice mail. While it won't eliminate busy signals or give your customers the options of voice mail, it will answer your phone when you are unavailable. Whether your preference if voice mail or answering machine, *do not leave a business line unanswered.* Your recorded voice on a machine is much less damaging to your business than a phone that rings, and rings and....

If you do use an answering machine, make certain that the recorded message is courteous, short, and professional. If the message is too long, chances are the person calling will not stay on the line long enough to leave a message.

The best answering machines provide remote answering, a feature that lets you call in for messages when you are away from your phone.

k. Time and tech

Somewhere between technophobia and technoaddiction lies the balance in making today's electronics work for you. For many people it is technology that allows them the choice of working from home. Others work at home to escape it. What cannot be denied is that you are doing business in a wildly competitive world. Your tasks are many and time is often scarce. Sometimes the going can get a little tough, particularly when everything depends on you. Practical use of technology can help. Conventional wisdom says that when you need a hand you will find it at the end of your arm. If that hand has the right tool, it is powerful indeed.

12

Taxation and
your home business

*It was as true...as turnips is. It was as true...as taxes is.
And nothing's truer than them.*

Charles Dickens

A small book that aims to help you plan and start your own business
cannot inform you on all aspects of taxation and the impact it will
have on your business. What it can do is promote tax awareness and
encourage you to become informed about the tax rules and regulations that will affect your enterprise.

It is no secret that many home-based businesses deliberately
maintain a cloak of invisibility in order to evade the tax collector.
Need I tell you that this is illegal? I hope not. The practice of tax evasion is a risky one. It is particularly so now, as the IRS and Revenue
Canada become increasingly aware, and very interested, in this
flourishing underground world.

Cheating on taxes may be a national pastime, but the penalties are
severe. If you are audited and charged with tax evasion, the amount
assessed as owing may well exceed what would have been due if
proper records were kept and the full tax paid in the first place. Not
only do you risk your business and perhaps your life savings, you
also destroy your integrity. Extreme cases risk heavy fines and im-
prisonment. Complain if you will when the tax collector bites, lobby
for change when the cause is just, but under no circumstances resort
to cheating and evasion.

a. Avoidance versus evasion

You can, with clear conscience, avoid paying undue taxes. Planning your financial affairs to ensure that you pay the smallest amount of tax possible is not illegal. It's plain good business.

The line between tax avoidance and tax evasion can get blurry at times. When it does, your accountant or tax planner is your greatest resource. It is his or her job to keep abreast of the latest tax rules, regulations, and allowable deductions. If you have any doubts about the tax implications of any business expense, check it out. Claiming ignorance when the auditor arrives is considered an offense not an excuse.

b. Starting smart

Treat your business as a business from the very beginning. Many people start their operations in a haphazard fashion. Perhaps they operate part time or run a hobby business. Because they make very few sales, and cash going out of the business greatly exceeds the cash coming in, they don't think much about the tax collector.

What they don't realize is that these early losses, if recorded properly, may be used to decrease taxes when they are showing a profit. If you are running an enterprise with the intent or expectation of profit, business losses can be deducted against income and provide a tax saving in future years. Play by the rules and you can turn those losses into money in your pocket.

To be a business in the eyes of the tax collector it is wise to look like a business. Don't intermingle personal records and business records. Running your personal and business activities from one checkbook is a mistake that can cost you valuable business deductions. Not only does it create confusion at tax time, but your business has a credibility problem which, should there be a dispute, would not be easily overcome. Open a separate bank account for your business and then use that account to deposit all income received from the business and to write all your checks. If you operate the business in your own name, this will save you from tax chaos.

Keep every receipt. You are entitled to claim expenses that relate to your business. To validate these expenses, keep all receipts and develop a good system for filing them. Over the life of your business, even small amounts add up, and the dollars saved in taxes can be substantial. The IRS in the United States and Revenue Canada are quick to disallow expenses that are not backed up with proper documentation.

c. *Expenses that require special attention*

While running your enterprise, you will incur expenses. These expenses, itemized and recorded properly, form the basis of your claim for deductions against your business income. Some expenses have come under close scrutiny by the tax collector in recent years, particularly those that are perceived to have an element of personal benefit. Examples of such expenses are homes, automobiles, and computers. While only a qualified professional can give definitive advice, here is a quick overview of this type of expense.

1. *Your home*

Generally speaking, you are allowed to deduct that portion of your house or apartment used for business purposes if it is your principal place of business. Also, your home office must be used exclusively by the business to earn business income. For example, you cannot use a room for a bedroom at night and an office during the day. The deductions include rent, mortgage interest, heating, electricity, and other expenses in a ratio to the area of the house used for the business. A good idea is to take measurements of your working area. Should you be questioned, generalities are not enough. Recent changes in both the U.S. and Canadian tax regulations governing home business deductions limit the allowable deductions to total income from the business. Deductions that have not been allowed in the current year may be carried forward to be claimed against future revenue. Check with your accountant.

Note: In both Canada and the United States, if you claim a deduction for depreciation of your home, you attract tax should you sell your home and make a profit. *Again, check with your accountant! Make certain you understand completely the tax impact of "business use of the home" regulations.*

2. *Your telephone*

Your business phone, as distinct from your personal phone, is a fully deductible expense as are all long-distance charges and telephone extensions used for business purposes. Having a business phone also is a clear indication to the tax department that you are in a credible business. Although some home operators use their personal line for business, it is not a good idea. Not only is it against most phone company regulations, in extreme cases you risk being assessed for past usage at the full business rate. If you are using your home telephone for business calls, keep a complete record of all long-distance expenses that are business related.

3. Your car

Automobile expenses that relate to business usage such as gasoline, repairs and maintenance, insurance, parking charges, etc. are deductible. For tax purposes, you must keep an accurate record of all such expenses. Create a car expense logbook where expenses, both business and personal, can be entered as they are incurred. Many business diaries contain such logs or you can prepare one yourself. Use Sample #6 as a model.

The business portion of your expense is calculated by dividing the total business miles driven by total miles driven in the year. Record everything — trips to the post office, customer calls, visits to your accountant or lawyer, picking up business parcels — everything. And don't forget receipts from parking lots. If it's business related, it is deductible.

Note that the tax department will not allow you to create logs or records of any kind "after the fact" to claim expenses. The only exception to this would be if the originals were destroyed by fire or act of nature.

4. Your computer

What is the difference between a taxidermist and a tax collector? The taxidermist takes only your skin.

Mark Twain

If you have a home computer that you use for business, you are able to deduct the business portion as an expense. The tax department assumes that a computer at home is used for both business and personal reasons. Because of this, you should keep a detailed record of your computer usage on a daily basis. This easily becomes routine if you keep the record book in a handy spot beside your computer. Logbooks for record keeping are available at some stationery and computer stores, or you can create one of your own using Sample #7 as a model. When you prepare those sales letters, enter your invoices, or do your business planning, write a description of what you are doing and the time spent. You don't have to do it to the minute; blocks of 15 minutes or so will be close enough.

Total your computer usage time every month on a summary sheet and file it for future reference. Proper records will ensure you the maximum deduction. Proof of computer usage also lets you deduct for computer and peripheral supplies such as forms, printer ribbons, diskettes, etc.

d. More allowable expenses

Many more expenses are allowable in your business, and all must be backed up with accurate and complete records. Fortunately, they are easier to account for than those mentioned above. Usually, you will receive an invoice addressed and directed to your business name. Once a month, you will sit down and write checks to the various suppliers that provide goods and services to your business. It is all straightforward. On those occasions when you do pay cash, be sure to get a receipt for your files that shows what the cash payment was for. Here is a list of more expenses that you are able to deduct:

(a) All licenses, dues, and subscriptions including your business license, memberships in business associations, business magazines, and trade journals.

(b) You can deduct all advertising costs, newspapers, magazines, brochures, etc.

(c) If you travel for business purposes, it is deductible. Airfares, hotels, and car rental are some examples. In both the United States and Canada, only a specified percentage of food costs are deductible, so keep those receipts. A diary or log book of travel expenses is good backup.

(d) Any office expense, from desk to paper clips, if it is intended for use in your operation, can be deducted. This includes those computer supplies, diskettes, ribbons, etc. as well as file folders, rubber stamps, staplers, and any other small items that you need to organize and run your enterprise. It also includes larger expenses such as furniture and filing cabinets.

(e) You can't go to a convention every week, but reasonable expenses relating to convention attendance is allowed.

(f) If you take out a loan for your business, the interest on that loan is an acceptable expense. The charges the bank makes on your account — cost of checks or special services, for example — are also deductible.

(g) Delivery and freight charges, including freight charges on your delivered inventory and supplies and the cost of shipping the product to your customer, are deductible.

Nothing hurts more than having to pay an income tax, unless it's not having to pay an income tax.

Thomas R. Dewar

Sample #6
Car expense record

Month:_____   Year:_____

Date	Business conducted	Speedometer Start	Stop	Total mileage	Parking exp. $	Oil/ gas $
_____	_____	_____	_____	_____	_____	_____
_____	_____	_____	_____	_____	_____	_____
_____	_____	_____	_____	_____	_____	_____
_____	_____	_____	_____	_____	_____	_____
_____	_____	_____	_____	_____	_____	_____
_____	_____	_____	_____	_____	_____	_____
_____	_____	_____	_____	_____	_____	_____
_____	_____	_____	_____	_____	_____	_____
_____	_____	_____	_____	_____	_____	_____
_____	_____	_____	_____	_____	_____	_____
_____	_____	_____	_____	_____	_____	_____
_____	_____	_____	_____	_____	_____	_____

Totals   _____ ____ ____

Total parking, gas, & oil =   _____

Other car expenses, repairs, etc.:
Date   Description   Amount
_____   _____   _____
_____   _____   _____

Total for month   _____

Sample #7
Computer usage log

Date:_____

Start	Time Stop	Total time	Description of use
_____	_____	_____	_____
_____	_____	_____	_____
_____	_____	_____	_____
_____	_____	_____	_____
_____	_____	_____	_____
_____	_____	_____	_____
_____	_____	_____	_____
_____	_____	_____	_____
_____	_____	_____	_____
_____	_____	_____	_____
_____	_____	_____	_____

Total time today   _____

(h) Business cards, stationery, or any other special forms needed for your business are standard deductions.

(i) If business is good and you decide to donate some of your profits to a charity, it is an allowable business expense.

(j) Payments on leased equipment are expensed in the month paid.

(k) All consultations with your lawyer and accountant are accepted business expenses. This includes preparation of your tax return.

(l) Some businesses have a higher-than-average need to purchase or subscribe to business related publications. Business or computer consultants are an example. All such publications are included as valid expenses to run the business.

(m) It is permissible to deduct the premium on your business insurance policy.

(n) Within reason, you can deduct the expense of gifts to your customers. This might be a gift at Christmas or a small token to commemorate a special event. Don't go overboard with this one as the tax department watches this expense closely.

(o) Courses to help you run your business and to update your skills are a legitimate expense, so if you plan on a bookkeeping course or computer seminar, keep records.

(p) There are new rules on entertainment deductions, such as taking a client out to lunch, in both Canada and the United States. Check this with your accountant. Within reason, as defined by the tax department, such expenses are acceptable.

(q) Employee wages are a normal expense for any business. If you employ someone either full time or part time, wages paid are deductible. You can also deduct expenses for services contracted for your business, such as janitorial or secretarial.

e. Tax information sources

Every business is different and many have expenses unique to them. In theory, if an expense is incurred for the benefit of the business, it is tax deductible. Like all theory, it has gray areas. If you are in doubt about what is and what is not an allowable expense for your business, check with your accountant. Another approach is to gain as much knowledge as possible.

In the United States, contact your local IRS office. They provide many helpful publications on all aspects of taxation for home and small business including *Tax Guide for Small Business, Taxpayer's Starting a Business*, and *Guide to Free Tax Services* (call toll-free 1-800-829-3676 for a copy). All of them and more are contained in *Your Business Tax Kit*, a must-have for anyone starting a new business. And check out the Small Business Tax Education Programs (STEP), a series of workshops and seminars done in partnership with various community education groups. Attendees of these workshops can sign up for *Tax Tips*, a monthly newsletter setting out tax information in non-technical language.

Want more information? Try 1-800-829-1040 and ask for a taxpayer education coordinator. They can fill you in on useful publications, seminars, and other services for business people looking for tax knowledge.

If you are on the Internet, drop in to the Department of the Treasury, *http://www.ustreas.gov* where you'll find more information than you'll ever need to know about tax.

In Canada, contact your local Revenue Canada office or call T.I.P.S., their automated phone service. You'll find the numbers listed in the Government of Canada section of your telephone book. Revenue Canada offers numerous publications covering all aspects of taxation as well as other services aid the fledgling business person. You can also visit their Web page at *http://www.revcan.ca.* Information about taxes can also be found through your Canada Business Service Centre.

Another source is your local library. There are many books on tax and small business, and they all contain valuable information that might save you money. Be sure to check the copyright dates of the books. Tax regulations undergo constant change, and last year's fact could be this year's fiction. Outdated tax information is not only misleading, it could be costly.

Your local bookstores probably carry a few of the many tax guides. Usually, the information is current and

"HOW WAS I TO KNOW YOU CHANGED THE GAME PLAN YESTERDAY?"

factual and the authors write in language that the layperson can understand. It doesn't hurt to spend a few hours a year reading about tax. It may not be as entertaining as a good novel, but it will help simplify conversations with your accountant at tax time.

You might also ask an accounting firm for help. All good accounting firms have published guides to tax, ranging from small pamphlets to small books. They are written clearly and are always current.

f. Tax planning

No person or business can ignore taxes. They are integral to our way of life and to the success or failure of business ventures. While most people believe that the only fair tax is the one the other person pays, you cannot escape paying your fair share.

The best way to come out on top, or, at the very least, avoid paying more tax than you have to, is to be aware of them and plan accordingly. You do not have to become a tax expert, but if you read, listen, and consult occasionally with a qualified tax expert, both you and your business will be the better for it.

13

Growing concerns

If you can look into the seeds of time,
And say which grain will grow
and which will not,
Speak.

a. Caring for your cash

To have a healthy business, cash must circulate within it on a regular and reliable basis. The need for cash and sensible cash management grows right along with your business. As it expands and you add more customers and incur more expenses, this becomes increasingly obvious.

If you haven't made the effort to plan your cash needs by doing a cash flow forecast (see chapter 6), you may be shocked at how quickly your cash goes out and how slowly the customers' cash comes in. You might be wondering how to finance your latest orders. It may seem to you that the more business you do the less cash you have. In fact, this is often true in a new and growing enterprise. If you have done some planning, you're not shocked and you do have money on hand to finance those new orders, but you quickly see that steps must be taken to increase the speed of the money coming in and slow down the amount of money going out.

Caring for your cash is both an administrative task and a financial responsibility. Making decisions early about credit policy and collection procedures will help ensure that your cash flows smoothly.

Making decisions early about credit policy and collection procedures will help ensure that your cash flows smoothly.

1. *Giving credit*

Businesses grant credit to their customers for various reasons. One of them is to increase sales. When you grant credit, your customer can buy goods or services that they would be unable to afford if they had to lay out cash. The second reason is *not to lose sales.* Credit is an accepted service when conducting business, and it is a benefit that most customers have come to expect. Given the choice of buying from a supplier that gives credit and one that doesn't, most customers will opt for the one that does. If you are in a business where granting credit is commonplace, you will probably lose customers if you don't follow the trend.

The disadvantages of selling on credit are —

  (a) the risk of not collecting,

  (b) the added administration of the collection process, and

  (c) the extension of time in which you do not realize a cash return for your goods or service.

Your money goes out long before your customer's money comes in. Because of this, you need more cash on hand than the business that deals strictly in cash.

Giving credit is also an added expense for your business. It is a loan to your customers. To grant that loan, you must establish their credit worthiness, keep special records, and develop a system to collect the amount due in the event they don't pay. You must also expect to have bad debts, which must be accounted for in your cash planning.

2. *The cash-only business*

The best way to run a business is on an all-cash basis. By doing this you limit the time between money going out for your enterprise (your payments for materials, supplies, labor, etc.) and money coming in. Because of this, you save money. You have none of the expenses associated with granting credit and you have no risk of bad debts. If you can operate on a cash basis without a severe loss of business, do so. Your business will be healthier for it and you will have much less stress.

b. Keeping the lid on credit

If your business is retail, and you are selling directly to the consumer, organize yourself to take bank cards. The charge for this service, when compared to the overhead costs (and headaches) of managing consumer credit, is worth it. There is almost no delay in receipt of cash from bank cards and the paperwork is minimal. You can get information on the rules and rates for Visa, MasterCard, etc. from local supporting banks or trust companies. Ask for their merchant information kit.

If you do business with other businesses, you may choose to offer credit either because your competitors do or because you see it as a quick way to increase the customer base of your operation. If you will be giving credit to other businesses, don't be haphazard. Business customers are also a risk. Many have a definite policy of not paying bills for 90 to 120 days. If you can't afford to extend credit for this length of time, you will want to know about such policies in advance. Start by planning a system to monitor your credit customers, and be zealous in maintaining it. There are various techniques that you can use to help.

1. Get a deposit

Asking for a deposit is an important technique, particularly if your operation is one in which you must buy to supply. Most customers are not reluctant to pay a deposit on orders for work that is material intensive. If you need to order special inventory or materials to fill a customer's order, ask for a deposit large enough to cover all or part of your cash outlay when the order is placed. This minimizes your risk in the event the customer does not pay.

2. Ask for a work-in-progress payment

Asking for a work-in-progress payment is a good policy for home businesses that primarily sell time. If work for a client will be done over an extended period, you can and should arrange for payment along the way. To be professional, prepare a report for the customer at each stage of the project, or when money is due, showing what is accomplished to date. This policy is a good one for long consulting contracts or other time-intensive service operations.

WHY IS THERE SO MUCH MONTH AT THE END OF THE MONEY?

(UNKNOWN)

3. *Bill promptly*

Bill instantly if you can. The sooner the invoice is in the hands of the customer the sooner your money will come in. Try to develop a system of billing that coincides with customer acceptance of the goods or the completion of service. Remember, if you delay billing, you delay receipt of the cash.

4. *Set clear payment terms*

Don't be slipshod about credit terms. Decide what terms and conditions are acceptable to you when giving credit and communicate them to your customer up front. Is payment due in 10 days or 30 days? Is the payment-due date calculated from date of goods received, date of invoice, or statement date? The basic terms and conditions should be shown clearly on your invoice. Don't forget to include a returns policy. Don't give the customer unlimited time to use (and abuse?) your goods and then return them.

5. *Check credit references*

You should always check credit references on your new customers. No one expects to be given credit without having their references checked. Ask for the customer's bank and the names of at least two other credit references — and check them out. If you are dealing with another business, ask for the names of at least two other suppliers and check their experience of doing business with your potential new customer. Your bank manager is also a good source for credit information on a potential customer.

If the order is a large one and needs a substantial outlay of your own cash to complete, consider calling a credit bureau. There will be a fee, but if you are very nervous about a new account, listen to your instincts, and do a thorough credit investigation. A fee is a small price to pay for a relaxed state of mind. You can also check with the Better Business Bureau. The BBB doesn't give out financial information, but it will provide basic information on a business. If that business has been the target of lawsuits or customer complaints, you may want to be cautious.

When it comes to bad debts, many small businesses are their own worst enemies because they do not take the time up front to check new accounts. Many of them are naive in thinking that collection problems belong to the "other guy" and won't happen to them. They may think the sale is so small it doesn't warrant taking the time for a credit check. Some are even afraid that asking about a customer's credit history is in some way insulting that person. Please remember that it is your cash on the line, and letting bad debts, even small ones, accumulate will drain the life from your business.

6. *Keep your customer information current*

This is necessary if credit is a routine part of your business. Unfortunately, you often can't spot bad debts until they are just that — bad. You have little or no chance of collecting such debts if you do not have up-to-date information. Make sure you have the full name and address of both the customer and his or her bank. File the information and make sure that you update it at least once a year to ensure the data is current.

7. *Plan your collection strategy*

Decide from the beginning what steps you will take to collect on overdue accounts and when you will take them. What you do should depend on how late the payment is. It is not necessary to send a stinging demand for payment to a customer who is 5 to 15 days late paying the bill. A friendly reminder like the one shown in Sample #8 is enough. On the other hand, when a customer is seriously overdue, you have reason to act strongly. Prepare some request-for-payment letters for such occasions. Be timely in reminding a customer that they have skipped a payment, and take firm steps to collect your money when the situation warrants it. Sample #9 is an example of such a letter.

Before writing the warning letter, be sure you have tried to communicate by phone. A personal call requesting payment is a powerful collection tool. Remember that after 90 days, your chance of collecting diminishes rapidly. Keep careful records of each step in the collection process and date them. This includes dates and notes on telephone calls.

8. *Put delinquent customers on a cash-only basis*

Do not continue to extend credit to long overdue accounts. If the customer wishes to continue doing business with you while in the overdue column, make sure you receive cash for newly shipped goods or services. While this step may seem logical to you, many small business people routinely give additional credit to late accounts. Their reasons vary: poor record keeping, lack of confidence to deal with the customer in a straightforward manner, or sympathy for a customer's cash problem. There may be occasions when a show of goodwill to a customer with temporary financial problems may encourage their

Sample #8
The polite reminder

June 2, 200-

Mr. J. Tolate
The Tardy Company Ltd.
123 Overdue Lane
Slow City, CA 98765

Dear Mr. Tolate:

Re: Invoice #99999, dated May 2, 200-.

Our records show that payment for the invoice noted above in the amount of $564.79 has not yet been received.

Have you overlooked it, or is there some problem that we should know about? Please call if there is some way we can be of help.

Yours truly,

F. M. Collecteur

F.M. Collecteur

P.S. If your check is in the mail, please disregard this letter.

Sample #9
Final notice letter

August 2, 200-

Mr. J. Tolate
The Tardy Company Ltd.
123 Overdue Lane
Slow City, CA 98765

Mr. Tolate:

Re: Overdue Account: Amount owing $564.79

We are sorry that you have not taken the action necessary to settle this account. As you have ignored both our previous letter and our telephone calls, we are left with no choice other than to turn the account over to our lawyer.

Please be advised that we will take legal action if payment is not received within seven days.

Yours truly,

F.M. Collecteur

future loyalty. Just be certain you can afford such generosity and know its limits.

9. *Act promptly on all overdue accounts*

This is the cardinal rule in credit collection. *You must act immediately.* Sending friendly reminders when an account is 90 days overdue will get you nowhere. When you see an account slip into the late column, take action right away. If you delay that action, the late-paying customer quickly becomes an uncollectible bad debt.

Customers have two reasons for not paying: either they can't or they won't. While most bad debts are the result of the former, there is an increasing tendency among businesses, big and small, to use the other person's cash by delaying payment as long as possible. The logic is simple; your money is cheaper than bank money. Banks not only expect payment on the borrowed money's principal, but also demand interest. More important, they have the clout to collect on both. That clout is collateral.

The small home-based enterprise does not have the same kind of influence. You are particularly at risk from the delayed-payment tactic if you are poorly organized or lackadaisical in your collection efforts. You stand a better chance of collecting your money sooner if you have a clear credit policy and a consistent approach to collection. If a customer understands that you are serious about your money and energetic about the job of collecting it, your invoice has a better chance of being paid. The homepreneur who does not have a planned collection process will be the one whose checks are forever "in the mail."

c. More tips on cash management

No man's credit is as good as his money.

Ed Howe

Prompt billing, a well-organized credit policy, and consistent collection procedures will help ensure that the cash coming into your business is timely. Here are a few more thoughts on how you can keep that cash working for you:

(a) Make deposits daily. Don't hold checks until it is convenient for you to go to the bank. If your bank is not close to your home, arrange for deposit privileges at a branch of your bank that is.

(b) Open an interest-bearing account. When you have excess cash, don't leave it in a current account that pays no interest. There is no reason for even the smallest amount of cash to sit idle. Make it work for you by earning interest.

(c) Pay bills only when due. Check the payment dates on all invoices that you receive, and don't pay before that date. Hold your own cash as long as possible without damaging your credit rating. The exception to this is if the supplier offers a discount for early payment. Such discounts can be worth taking advantage of.

(d) Don't prepay unless you must. Whenever you can, work on a pay-as-you-go basis. As a start-up enterprise, you may have trouble avoiding some prepayments because you don't have a track record with suppliers, but it is not necessary to make it a habit. When you have been in business for a few months, ask your current supplier or any new suppliers to drop prepayment requirements and establish a full credit relationship.

(e) Sell off slow-moving inventory. The purpose of your inventory is to provide cash for your enterprise. If you have outdated, stagnant inventory, make every effort to sell it. Offer sale prices, discounts, or whatever it takes to turn those goods into cash as quickly as possible. Old inventory doesn't get any younger left sitting on the shelf, and it sure doesn't help your bank balance.

(f) Never purchase what you don't need. Always use your cash wisely. Give thought to how you spend it and on what. Conserve cash by getting competitive bids whenever you can. Regularly take time to analyze your business expenditures. Check the prices you are paying for office supplies, stationery, etc. Could you get them for less somewhere else?

(g) Keep proper records and use them. When it comes to cash you should always know exactly where you and your business stand. You can't do this unless you have a record-keeping system that allows you to monitor your accounts receivable and payable. If you have a good accounting system, such reports are available. Review them on a regular basis and take action when necessary.

d. Staying put

People who work at home are there because they want to be. They have bypassed the traditional office in favor of working from home, and home is where they want to stay. A reader survey conducted by *Home Office Computing* magazine confirms this. A poll of 4,000 of their readers found that 100% were happier at home than in the conventional work environment, and that while 81% wanted their businesses to grow, only 12% wanted to move it out of their home.

If you want to continue running your business at home, too much success can be a problem. Most of the difficulty centers on having too little space. Perhaps you have so many orders you need to carry more inventory. The demands for your services may exceed your personal ability, and you need to hire employees. Perhaps the zoning in your area restricts hiring anyone other than family members. The business may have gradually taken over your house to the point that having friends for dinner becomes impossible because you can't find your dining room table under the stacks of paper and supplies. When you are just starting your enterprise, you probably can't conceive of problems like these. They do happen.

When they do, you think you must choose between limiting your growth or moving your business to space outside the home. But if home is where your business heart is, there are alternatives.

Some homepreneurs simply move to a bigger house — one large enough to let them grow their business and remain at home. While this is an option for some, it won't work for others whose business is dependent for its success on its current location. For a secretarial service that has carefully developed a customer base in the local community, for example, it might mean starting from scratch. If you plan to keep your business at home, regardless of its success, you might consider the following suggestions:

(a) Make your home office corporate and rent space for employees and production. Some homepreneurs keep the accounting, administration, and sales functions at home and hire outside space for employees or production.

   If you are accustomed to being a hands-on manager, this method can be a difficult adjustment. You will have to develop definite checks and balances to ensure quality control. Consider making one of your employees the supervisor at the out-of-home site so that you have a direct line of communication.

(b) Use mini-storage for surplus inventory. I recommend this to any person whose business is inventory intensive. If need for storage is driving you out of your house, this may be the easiest way to solve the problem. Renting even a small space outside your home may give you back space enough to add more capacity to your business.

(c) Contract out. (For legalities, see chapter 5.) By contracting out part of your operation on a regular basis, you can save space and maintain the autonomy of working from your home. You could choose to contract for product packaging, for example, or some other facet of production that is easily segmented from the main process. If you are prepared to contract with another person or business on this basis, you can more easily negotiate a price break.

   If you choose contracting out as a means of keeping your business at home, select the contractor carefully. Be certain he or she understands completely the standard of quality you expect. Monitor the contractor's output.

(d) Put an addition on your present home. If business is good enough, why not? This alternative depends entirely on your personal judgment and the potential of your home. But if you are determined to stay at home and want your business right under your nose where you can be sure it runs exactly the way you want it to, this is the best solution. If you do decide that adding to your home will work for you, please be sure that such an addition does not affect the resale value of your home. A home radically customized to accommodate the special needs of a business loses appeal in the eyes of the potential home buyer.

The decision to keep your business at home or move on will ultimately be up to you. Your family, personal feelings, business goals, and lifestyle will all come into play when the time comes to make such a choice.

e. Success — your way

As a homepreneur, you will measure success by your own yardstick. You will shape your own lifestyle, calculate your own risk, and choose your own path. It is a heady and enjoyable experience. Will there be challenges? Yes. Problems? Yes. But they are easily met — and bested — by using creativity, a little wit, and a goodly share of plain old common sense. No doubt you have a fair measure of each.

Success in business can be yours, and you can have it on *your* terms. The way is plain — work hard, work smart, and work at home.

May you achieve — and enjoy — the goals you seek.

Appendix 1
Government names and addresses

a. United States

1. State departments offering business assistance

Alabama Development Office
401 Adams Avenue
Montgomery, AL 36130
(205) 242-0400

Alaska Department of Commerce and Economic Development
Division of Business Development
P.O. Box D
Juneau, AK 99811-0800
(907) 465-2017

Arizona Department of Commerce
3800 North Central
Suite 1500
Phoenix, AZ 85012
(602) 280-1306

Arkansas Industrial Development Commission
Small Business Programs
One State Capital Mall
Little Rock, AR 72201
(501) 682-5275

California Department of Commerce Office of Small Business
801 K Street, Suite 1600
Sacramento, CA 95814
(916) 324-1295

Colorado Small Business Center
Office of Business Development
1625 Broadway, Suite 1710
Denver, CO 80202
(303) 892-3809
Toll-free in state: (800) 333-7798

Connecticut Department of Economic Development
Small Business Services
865 Brock Street
Hartford, CT 06067-3405
(203) 258-4200

Delaware Development Office
99 Kings Highway
P.O. Box 1401
Dover, DE 19903
(302) 739-4271

District of Columbia Office of Business and Economic Development
717-14th Street, N.W.
10th Floor
Washington, DC 20005
(202) 727-6600

Florida Department of Commerce
Bureau of Business Assistance
443 Collins Building
107 W. Gaines Street
Tallahassee, FL 32399-2000
(904) 487-9357

Georgia Department of Community Affairs
Community and Economic Development Section
1200 Equitable Building
100 Peachtree Street,
Atlanta, GA 30303
(404) 656-3872

*Hawaii Department of Business, Economic
Development, and Tourism*
Business Services Division
Grosvenor Center, Mauka Tower
737 Bishop Street, Suite 1900
Honolulu, HI 96804
(808) 586-2591

Idaho Department of Commerce
Economic Development Division
700 West State Street
Boise, ID 83720
(208) 334-2470

*Illinois Department of Commerce and
Community Affairs*
SBDC Program
620 East Adams Street, 5th Floor
Springfield, IL 62701
(217) 524-5856

Indiana Small Business Development Corporation
One North Capitol Avenue, Suite 1275
Indianapolis, IN 46204
(317) 264-2820

Iowa Department of Economic Development
Small Business Bureau
200 East Grand Avenue
Des Moines, IA 50309
(515) 242-4758
Toll-free in state: (800) 532-1216

Kansas Department of Commerce
400 S.W. 8th Street, 5th Floor
Topeka, KS 66603-3957
(913) 296-3480

Kentucky Cabinet for Economic Development
Division of Small Business
2300 Capital Plaza Tower
Frankfort, KY 40601
(502) 564-7140

Louisiana Department of Economic Development
P.O. Box 94185
Baton Rouge, LA 70804
(504) 342-5388

*Maine Department of Economic and
Community Development*
Office of Business Development
State House Station #59
Augusta, ME 04333
(207) 289-3153

*Maryland Department of Economic and
Employment Development*
Division of Business Development
Redwood Towers, 10th Floor
217 East Redwood Street
Baltimore, MD 21202
(301) 333-6985

Massachusetts Office of Business Development
Business Services Division
Room 2101, One Ashburton Place
Boston, MA 02108
(617) 727-3206

Michigan Department of Commerce
P.O. Box 30004
Lansing, MI 48909
(517) 373-6241

Minnesota Small Business Assistance Office
900 American Center Building
150 East Kellogg Blvd.
St. Paul, MN 55101
(612) 296-3871

*Mississippi Department of Economic and
Community Development*
Business Assistance Division
P.O. Box 849
Jackson, MS 39205
(601) 359-3552

Missouri Department of Economic Development
Business Development Section
Truman State Office Building
P.O. Box 118
Jefferson City, MO 65102
(314) 751-9055

Montana Department of Commerce
Business Development Division
1424 Ninth Avenue
Helena, MT 59620
(406) 444-3923

Nebraska Department of Economic Development
P.O. Box 94666
301 Centennial Mall South
Lincoln, NE 68509-4666
(402) 471-4167
Toll-free in state: (800) 426-6505

Nevada Office of Small Business
Commission on Economic Development
3770 Howard Hughes Parkway, Suite 295
Las Vegas, NV 89158
(702) 486-7282

*New Hampshire Office of Business and
Industrial Development*
172 Pembroke Road
Concord, NH 03302-0856
(603) 271-2591

*New Jersey Department of Commerce
and Economic Development*
Division of Development for Small Businesses and
  Women and Minority Businesses
20 West State Street, CN 835
Trenton, NJ 08625
(609) 292-3860

New Mexico Economic Development Department
Economic Development Division
1100 St. Francis Drive
Santa Fe, NM 87503
(505) 827-0380

New York Department of Economic Development
Division for Small Business
1515 Broadway, 51st Floor
New York, NY 10036
(212) 827-6140

North Carolina Department of Commerce
Small Business Development
  and Technology Center
4509 Creedmoor Road, Suite 201
Raleigh, NC 27612
(919) 571-4154

*North Dakota Department of Economic
Development and Finance*
1833 East Bismarck Expressway
Bismarck, ND 58504
(701) 224-2810

Ohio Department of Development
Small Business Development Center
30 East Broadway Street
P.O. Box 1001
Columbus, OH 43266
(614) 466-2711
Toll-free in state: (800) 848-1300

Oklahoma Department of Commerce
Small Business Assistance Office
6601 Broadway Extension
Oklahoma City, OK 73116
(405) 843-9770

Oregon Economic Development Department
Office of Small Business Assistance
775 Summer Street, N.E.
Salem, OR 97310
(503) 373-1241
Toll-free in state: (800) 233-3306

Pennsylvania Department of Commerce
Office of Enterprise Development
401 Forum Building
Harrisburg, PA 17120
(717) 783-8950

Puerto Rico Department of Commerce
P.O. Box S-4275
San Juan, PRT 00905
(809) 724-3290

Rhode Island Department of Economic Development
Business Development Division
7 Jackson Walkway
Providence, RI 02903
(401) 277-2601

South Carolina Office of Small and Minority Business Assistance
Edgar A. Brown Building
1205 Pendleton Street, Room 441
Columbia, SC 29201
(803) 734-0562

South Dakota Governor's Office for Economic Development
711 East Wells Avenue
Pierre, SD 57501-3369
(605) 773-5032

Tennessee Department of Economic and Community Development
320 6th Avenue North
7th Floor
Nashville, TN 37243-0405
(615) 741-2626
Toll-free in state: (800) 872-7201

Texas Department of Commerce
816 Congress Avenue
P.O. Box 12728
Austin, TX 78711
(512) 472-5059

Utah Department of Economic Development — Small Business
324 South State Street, Suite 500
Salt Lake City, UT 84111
(801) 538-8775

Vermont Department of Economic Development
109 State Street
Montpelier, VT 05602
(802) 828-3221

Virgin Islands Small Business Development Agency
P.O. Box 6400
St. Thomas, VI 00601
(809) 774-8784

Virginia Department of Economic Development
Small Business and Financial Services
P.O. Box 798
Richmond, VA 23206-0798
(804) 371-8100

Washington Department of Trade and Economic Development
Business Assistance Center
919 Lakeridge Way, S.W., Suite A
Olympia, WA 98502
(206) 586-3021

West Virginia Governor's Office of Community and Industrial Development
Small Business Development Center
  Division
1115 Virginia Street East
Charleston, WV 25301
(304) 348-2960

Wisconsin Department of Development
123 West Washington Avenue
P.O. Box 7970
Madison, WI 53707
(608) 266-7099

Wyoming Division of Economic and Community Development
Herschler Building, 2nd Floor West
Cheyenne, WY 82002
(307) 777-7284

Note: Many states operate Small Business Development Centers. Such centers are based at universities and offer programs that are organized and cofinanced by the Small Business Administration. Participating universities provide faculty and counseling to small business owners and offer seminars covering topics such as marketing, managing, and financing a small business. Check with your local SBA office for more information.

2. Small Business Administration Information Office

Small Business Administration (Central)
409 3rd Street, S.W.
Washington, DC 20416
Toll-free: (800) 827-5722

To order publications, write —
Small Business Administration Publications
P.O. Box 30
Denver, CO 20415

b. Canada

A cooperative venture between governments (both federal and provincial) and nongovernment organizations, Canadian Business Service Centres (CBSCs) provide information and services designed to help Canadian businesses.

1. Alberta

The Business Link
100-10237 104th Street
Edmonton, AB T5J 1B1
(403) 422-7788
Toll-free: 1-800-272-9675
E-mail: bscedm@edmcbsc.ic.gc.ca

2. British Columbia

Canada/BC Business Service Centre
601 W. Cordova Street
Vancouver, BC V6G 1G1
(604) 775-5525
Toll-free: 1-800-667-2272

3. Manitoba

Canada Business Service Centre (Manitoba)
P.O. Box 2609
8th Floor, 330 Portage Avenue
Winnipeg, MB R3C 4B3
(204) 945-2456
Toll-free: 1-800-665-2019

4. Newfoundland

Canada Business Service Centre (Newfoundland)
90 O'Leary Avenue
P.O. Box 8687
St. John's, NF A1B 3T1
(709) 772-6022
Toll-free: 1-800-668-1010

5. New Brunswick

Canada/New Brunswick Business Service Centre
570 Queen Street
Fredericton, NB E3B 6Z6
(506) 444-6140
Toll-free: 1-800-668-1010

6. Northwest Territories

Canada/NWT Business Service Centre
3rd Floor, Northern United Place
5004-54th Street
Yellowknife, NT X1A 2L9
(403) 873-7958
Toll-free: 1-800-661-0599
E-mail: yel@cbsc.ic.gc.ca

7. Nova Scotia

Canada/Nova Scotia Business Service Centre
1575 Brunswick Street
Halifax, NS B3J 2G1
(902) 426-8604
Toll-free: 1-800-661-1010
E-mail: halifax@cbsc.ic.gc.ca

8. *Ontario*

Canada-Ontario Business Call Centre
(416) 954-4636
Toll-free: 1-800-567-2345
E-mail: cobcc@cbsc.ic.gc.ca

9. *Prince Edward Island*

Canada/PEI Business Service Centre
75 Fitzroy Street
P.O. Box 40
Charlottetown, PE C1A 7K2
(902) 368-0771
Toll-free: 1-800-661-1010

10. *Quebec*

Info Entrepreneurs (Quebec)
5 Place Ville Marie, Suite 12500
Montreal, QC H3B 4Y2
(514) 496-4636
Toll-free: 1-800-322-4636

11. *Saskatchewan*

Canada/Saskatchewan Business Service
    Centre
122-3rd Avenue N.
Saskatoon, SK S7K 2H6
(306) 956-2323
Toll-free: 1-800-667-4374

12. *Yukon*

Business Development Office
Department of Economic Development
P.O. Box 2703
Whitehorse, Yukon
Y1A 2C6
(403) 667-3011

Appendix 2
Good reading for the new homepreneur

a. General reading

Arden, Lynie. *The Work-at-Home Sourcebook.* Boulder, Colorado: Live Oak Publications, 1988.

Brabec, Barbara. *Homemade Money: The Definitive Guide to Success in a Home Business.* Whitehall, Virginia: Betterway Publications, 1992.

Cornish, Clive. *Basic Accounting for the Small Business.* Vancouver: Self-Counsel Press, 1992.

Davidson, Peter. *Earn Money at Home.* New York: McGraw-Hill Paperbacks, 1982.

Delaney, George, and Sandra Delaney. *The #1 Home Business Book.* Cockeysville, Maryland: Liberty House, 1981.

Edwards, Paul, and Sarah Edwards. *Working from Home: Everything You Need to Know about Living and Working under the Same Roof.* New York: Tarcher/St. Martin's Press, 1987.

Gray, Doug, and Diana Gray. *Home Inc.: The Canadian Home Based Business Guide.* Toronto: McGraw Hill, 1989.

Kahn, Sharon, and the Philip Lief Group. *101 Best Businesses to Start.* New York: Doubleday, 1988.

Levinson, Jay Conrad. *Guerrilla Marketing: Secrets for Making Big Profits from Your Small Business.* Boston: Houghton Mifflin Company, 1984.

Sullivan, George. *Work Smart, Not Hard.* New York: Facts on File Publications, 1987.

Taylor, Harold L. *Making Time Work for You.* Toronto: Stoddart Publishing Co., Ltd., 1989.

Whitmyer, Claude, Salli Rasberry, and Michael Phillips. *Running a One-person Business.* Berkeley, California: Ten Speed Press, 1989.

b. Reference

The Encyclopedia of Associations
Gale Research Company
Trade Shows and Exhibits Guide
633 Third Avenue, 34th Floor
New York, NY 10002

For their guide to upcoming shows in the U.S. and overseas, call toll-free 1-800-624-6283.